From Defiance
to Cooperation

From Defiance to Cooperation

Real Solutions for Transforming the
Angry, Defiant, Discouraged Child

John F. Taylor, Ph.D.

PRIMA PUBLISHING

Published by Prima Publishing, Roseville, California. Member of the Crown Publishing Group, a division of Random House, Inc., New York.

PRIMA PUBLISHING and colophon are trademarks of Random House, Inc., registered with the United States Patent and Trademark Office.

All of the characters in this book are based on real persons, but in some cases, names have been omitted or changed to protect the privacy of the people involved. Therefore, any resemblance to actual persons, living or dead, is purely coincidental, unless authorized by the actual person mentioned.

Illustrations by Tom McLelland.

Library of Congress Cataloging-in-Publication Data
Taylor, John F.
    From defiance to cooperation : real solutions for transforming the angry, defiant, discouraged child / John F. Taylor.
        p.   cm.
    Includes bibliographical references and index.
    ISBN 0-7615-2955-1
    1. Oppositional defiant disorder in children—treatment. 2. Oppositional defiant disorder in adolescence—treatment. 3. Child psychotherapy. I. Title.
RJ506.O66 T39   2001
618.92'8914—dc21   2001036263

03 04 05 06 HH 10 9 8 7 6 5 4 3
Printed in the United States of America
First Edition

Visit us online at www.primapublishing.com

To Brian and Dana, whose oppositional natures have been both a blessing and a challenge to us, their parents, and to them.

CONTENTS

INTRODUCTION

D O YOU DEAL with a "difficult" kid? Then I wrote this book just for you. It presents hundreds of specific, practical suggestions for improving life with a contrary, oppositional, power-seeking, defiant, rebellious, or argumentative child.

Whether you're a parent, a teacher, a counselor, a youth-group leader, or a concerned relative, dealing with an oppositional child is nerve-racking. On a good day. On a bad day, it's exhausting, defeating, dramatic, and sometimes even terrifying.

Nobody has all the answers, or even very many, to these types of parenting issues. But I have more than a few, and I'm happy to share them with you.

The answers I have for you work. They are honest, sensible, easy to implement, and intensely practical. They apply to any age child or teen and even to young adults. My focus is on rebuilding harmony in your family and within your personal relationship with any oppositional child. These ideas restore love, full and vibrant, in your family dynamics. That's what you'll find in this book, cover to cover.

What you won't find are techniques that send you deeper into conflict and further into the quicksand of power struggles. You will find no elaborate "behavior modification" schemes, no plans to administer rewards on a chart with stars and stickers that leave your oppositional child scoffing behind your back. You will find no recommendation for using lengthy periods of time-out or for ignoring your child's antics. Nor will you find recommendations for harsh, punishment-oriented clamping down on the child. If you want such guidance, you'll have to find another parenting book. There are plenty that advocate such approaches. I have no desire to keep you in the ignore-nag-yell-punish cycle. I'm going to get you out of it.

Some Special Terms for Special Children

Throughout this book, I use the word *child* broadly to indicate any child, teenager, or young adult. Sometimes, I specify a particular age group, such as young child or teenager.

In addition, I use the terms "oppositional child" and "oppositionality" as shorthand ways of indicating any child who demonstrates significant levels of defiance. Oppositionality appears in a range: from persistent defiance to diagnosable oppositional defiant disorder (ODD) to full-blown conduct disorders. The advice in this book is geared for parents and other adults who must supervise, care for, or counsel defiant children across that scale.

If you happen to be receiving professional help from a counselor or therapist who advocates a "behavior modification" approach, you can still integrate this book as a source of additional help. Simply use it to supplement, not replace, the guidance you are receiving.

You can use this book as the resource for a parent discussion class. There are study and discussion questions in appendix B. I encourage you to take advantage of this feature. You can easily integrate this book into just about any parent education discussion program, whether or not organized by a mental health or medical professional. There is no need for a professional leader; you can use this book as the reference, with the aid of the study questions. A.D.D. Plus has numerous related materials available to help put together a parent discussion type of parent education program. At the end of this introduction is contact information.

As I have traveled throughout the United States and Canada presenting seminars and providing training on attention deficit hyperactivity disorder (ADHD) and oppositional defiant disorder (ODD), I have talked with hundreds of parents who are near their wit's end trying to cope with the family-splitting pressure that occurs from an ODD child. I've learned many helpful techniques from these same parents, who have left no stone unturned in their efforts to find answers.

Just as I have imparted family-saving help to those parents and at the same time have received many helpful ideas from them, I hope to have the same impact for your benefit. Please use this book for its full potential. There is not a single lame idea in this book. They all work, though not universally in every setting with every parent and every oppositional child. Use whatever seems the best choice for you. And if you have found an additional idea not included in this book, please share it with me, so I can incorporate it.

In chapter 1, I attempt to make sense out of the mystery of why your child or teen shows an oppositional nature. The ultimate reason for excess plays for power is fear, in turn based on various reasons, of not having enough power. Unhealthy emotional experiences are often in the background of oppositional children. Competition within the family pours additional gasoline onto the fire of defiant misbehavior.

Chapter 2 reveals the three cardinal messages defiant children broadcast to the world and the six different forms of oppositional power-oriented misbehavior they show. You will learn to spot many additional aspects of oppositionality that perhaps you had not noticed before. I show you how impatience, hostility, self-centeredness, irritability, substance abuse, and other identifiable clusters of negative behavior fit into the picture. I also provide for you the current psychiatric definition of oppositional defiant disorder.

In chapter 3, I introduce the importance of opening up new, safer avenues through which the oppositional child can express needs and wants. You'll learn how to bolster your child's sense of belonging and of feeling strong and powerful in prosocial, appropriate ways. I show you many ways to upgrade the emotional tone within your family to create a new level of harmony and peace.

Chapter 4 details one of the main emphases needed in order to eliminate oppositional misbehavior. I help you form a truly effective bond of psychological intimacy with your child, removing the usefulness of defiance. You'll learn mistakes to avoid as well as techniques to use in freeing up emotional communication and decreasing oppositionality within your family.

Confronting a power-oriented child or teen is a crucial aspect of rebuilding harmony in your family. Chapter 5 gives what to say so your child will really listen and stop being defiant. I'll show you how to deal with lying, obtain agreements instead of arguments, and get around roadblocks like "I don't know" and "I don't care" from your child.

The ultimate purpose of discipline is to teach conscience-based self-control. Chapter 6 shows you how to put the emphasis on preventing misbehavior and power struggles in the first place rather than relying on outdated after-the-fact methods. I also show you the best types of responses to give after misbehavior has occurred, in order to assure better learning for next time and decreased oppositionality. The best way to handle your child's bullheadedness is to aim it in a better direction. In what *constructive* ways can your children use all that energy and determination?

Chapter 7 tells you how to channel your child's traits into socially acceptable, useful directions and away from being oppositional. Being a leader at school or in the neighborhood, gaining a sense of power by constructing an art project or performing on a stage, and dozens of other avenues are available. I'll help you find the avenues that are just right for your child and your family.

Most of my counseling with ODD children and teens has been with those who also carry a diagnosis of attention deficit hyperactivity disorder. ODD is the most common condition that overlaps with ADHD. My extensive experience in the field of ADHD has yielded an encyclopedic array of techniques that, in one way or another, affect the oppositional component of ADHD. Those techniques involve various nutritional options, prescribed medication, and the entire content of this book. I've produced numerous resources to assist with both ADHD and ODD. Please feel free to visit the Web site www.ADD-Plus.com. Mail requests for a catalog of ODD and ADHD resources to A.D.D. Plus, P.O. Box 4326, Salem OR 97302, or send an e-mail to addplus@hotmail.com.

Oppositional children are born leaders. Feast upon the hundreds of ideas in this book. They will bring a new dimension of release and a harnessing of your child's potential for successful adjustment. Enjoy!

1

Why Your Child Craves Power

B EN WAS A handsome child. Tall, dark-haired, green-eyed—adults and children alike were naturally attracted to him. Until they spent a few minutes in his company.

Even as a newborn, Ben seemed oppositional. When his mother attempted to comfort the crying child, he screamed and kicked and pushed away. When adults tried to cuddle or hold him, he squirmed and twisted to be put back down.

As he grew, so did his defiant behavior. During his first 4 years, his parents were asked to remove him from seven different day-care facilities. At the age of 4, he began slipping out of his family's house late at night to visit with neighbors. By the time he entered school, his more compliant younger siblings were terrified of being alone in a room with Ben. He had a string of enemies from preschool, and there wasn't a child in the neighborhood who cared to visit Ben's house.

His parents hoped school would allow Ben to start over with a clean slate. But year after year, he defied teachers, skipped classes, refused to do homework, and got himself suspended for oppositional behavior, defiance, and fighting.

The teenage years nearly tore his family apart. He began stealing from his parents and disappearing for two or three days at a time. Ben openly defied family rules, and when his parents would respond by grounding him or taking away his transportation, Ben would react by vandalizing the house. He alienated would-be friends with his bossiness, lack of cooperation, and disrespectful comments. At 16, he got his first job but was fired within two months for stealing. When he turned 17, his parents gave him the option of following rules or joining the army. He joined the army, but his oppositional defiance didn't mix with army rules, and after six months he was discharged for "failure to adapt."

> The oppositional child or teen wants power—too much of it and in all the wrong places.

Now that Ben's no longer living at home, he and his family are working out a better relationship. He is learning to recognize and change the destructive behavioral patterns he's adopted. The home he grew up in is no longer a chaotic, painful place to visit. And yes, he still backslides from time to time as he discovers how tough it is to make it as a young adult in a world that demands respect, responsible behavior, and adherence to rules.

The oppositional child or teen wants power—too much of it and in all the wrong places. Oppositional children are demanding. Their opposition to every reasonable request sucks the energy and patience out of their parents, their teachers, their coaches, and their caregivers. Those who interact with oppositional children say that in any given group of children— a family, a classroom, or a team—the oppositional child ends up receiving the lion's share of the discipline, attention, and energy of the responsible adult.

Not every oppositional child is as difficult as Ben. But some are even tougher. Oppositional children—particularly those who are diagnosed with oppositional defiant disorder (ODD) or its more severe sequel, conduct disorder (CD)—are at high risk for addictions, abusive behavior, and involvement with the penal system.

Hope for the Future

IS THERE HOPE? There is. Whether you're a parent, a caregiver, a teacher, or a friend, you can find peace, cooperation, and—yes—even tranquillity as you interact with a poweroriented, strong-willed child or teen.

As an adult dealing with an oppositional child, your own responses and behaviors can have a tremendous impact on the defiant behaviors and the power plays of children and teens with ODD. Moreover, by educating yourself about these disorders, you can learn to resolve difficulties that typically occur with any degree of defiant behavior.

In this book, I will help you understand your oppositional child and offer advice and optimism for creating a peaceful, loving relationship.

How long will it take? In general, the less severe the diagnosis, the more quickly and effectively you'll regain control over the chaotic world of living with an oppositional child. But even in severe cases of defiance, the advice in this book can bring about an immediate improvement in your own responses to behaviors that drive you crazy!

The Basics

SIMPLY PUT, AN oppositional child has an overdeveloped need to experience personal power. This need arises from any combination of three different circumstances: One source is the child's life experiences. The other two are brain structure and chemistry. These physical features have as their source both inherited temperament and toxic chemical upsets of brain formation and function.

Some children are born with a basic oppositional nature. Strong-willed from infancy, they have probably inherited certain hormonal and brain chemistry factors that create a power-seeking temperament.

Other children—who might not otherwise be afflicted with an oppositional temperament—suffer the misfortune of toxic attacks on their developing brains while they are still in the womb. Researchers are now learning that *in utero* influences can emerge years later as oppositional defiant disorder, attention deficit hyperactivity disorder (ADHD), and conduct disorder. Some of those toxins may originate from environmental and genetic conditions. Others are introduced through substances ingested while the child is developing. One recent study of nearly 2,800 young children found that smoking by expectant mothers is correlated with oppositional and defiant tendencies in their children. Prenatal marijuana smoking and alcohol use have also come under suspicion as factors contributing to abnormalities in brain structure and chemistry leading to oppositional defiant disorder.

ODD Plus Hyperactivity

OPPOSITIONAL TENDENCIES OCCUR with high frequency in children and teens who have various diagnosable disorders of behavior and performance, including a collection of conditions known as communication and learning disorders.

Oppositional defiant disorder is difficult to cope with all on its own. When it appears with additional behavioral disorders, it can tear families apart.

Attention deficit hyperactivity disorder is one of the most frequent disorders to appear with ODD. In 1979, I wrote the very first book devoted extensively to the family relationship issues of raising a child with ADHD. Since that time, I have focused extensively on various aspects of ADHD in my writings, seminars, and audio and video resources. Oppositional defiant disorder is a big part of the ADHD story.

Approximately 60 percent of teens with ADHD also have serious oppositional tendencies, and the majority of children and teens with ODD probably also have ADHD. So great is the overlap between these two conditions that oppositional defiant disorder is the single most frequent other diagnosis ascribed to hyperactive children. Often, young children who later develop this psychiatric diagnosis were emotionally volatile and physically hyperactive during the preschool years—two key indicators of ADHD.

> The majority of children and teens with oppositional defiant disorder probably also have attention deficit hyperactivity disorder.

Children and teens with ADHD are diagnosed as being of the hyperactive-impulsive type, the inattentive type, or the combined type (both hyperactive and inattentive). The two categories that include hyperactivity are the most likely to develop oppositional tendencies.

You can use the Taylor Hyperactivity Screening Checklist on the following page as a quick guide to whether or not a particular child is diagnosably hyperactive and therefore at risk for strong oppositional tendencies. A screening checklist should never be considered a substitute for a professional diagnosis. However, this one is very accurate for initial differentiating of children and teens with true hyperactivity from others of the same age.

A Hyperactivity Screening Checklist

THIS CHECKLIST MAKES a preliminary division between hyperactivity and other behavior problems. It is not a comprehensive list of all symptoms but lists the most observable differentiating symptoms—those likely to occur in hyperactive individuals and unlikely to occur in nonhyperactive individuals. Experience with this scale over the years has indicated that it is accurate from age 2 through adulthood. The items lean rather significantly in the direction of the fidgetiness and hyperactivity component of the ADHD syndrome, which is highly correlated with oppositionality.

For each of the 21 behaviors, put an X in one of the three boxes to show the typical behavior. Rate the behavior when the child or teen is not being supervised, helped, or reminded; when not watching television or a computer screen; and when not receiving any kind of treatment to control behavior.

Indicate the trend. Try to avoid Column B ratings; a 51-percent trend in either direction should merit an A or C rating.

Children whose oppositionality comes as an aspect of their ADHD are physiologically driven into their oppositionality. To become oppositional means, in part, to surrender some aspects of conscience. The combination of ADHD and oppositional

THE TAYLOR HYPERACTIVITY SCREENING CHECKLIST

For each of the 21 behaviors, put an X in one of the three boxes to show the typical behavior. Rate the behavior when the child or teen is not being supervised, helped, or reminded; not watching television or a computer screen; and not receiving any kind of treatment to control behavior.

Indicate the trend. Try to avoid column B ratings; a 51 percent trend in either direction should merit an A or C rating. Compared with others of approximately the same age, this child typically shows behavior:

A. Somewhat more like this	B. Absolutely no trend	C. Somewhat more like this		A. Somewhat more like this	B. Absolutely no trend	C. Somewhat more like this
1. Quiet person		Noisy and talkative person		12. Obeys authority, concerned about consequences		Defies authority, has "I don't care" attitude about consequences
2. Voice volume is soft or average		Voice is generally too loud for the situation		13. Trustable, follows through, obeys directions		Disobedient, forgetful, needs reminding to ensure compliance
3. Few mouth or body noises		Noisy, makes clicks, whistles, hums, cracks knuckles		14. Calm, emotionally stable, has mild or slow mood changes		Moody, unpredictable, quick to anger or tears
4. Walks at appropriate times		Flits around, runs ahead, needs to be called back, is jumpy		15. Easygoing, handles frustration without much anger, is patient, can be teased		Inflexible, irritable, impatient, easily frustrated
5. Keeps hands to self		Pokes, touches, feels, grabs		16. Intensity of displayed emotion is mild or moderate		Emotions are extreme and poorly controlled; no "damper pedal" on emotion; explosive, has tantrums
6. Appears calm, can be still		Always has a body part moving, fidgets with hands or feet, is squirmy		17. Cooperative, obeys and enforces rules of work and play		Oppositional; complains about rules, routines, or chores; wants to be the exception
7. Can just sit		Has to be doing something to occupy self when sitting, is quickly bored		18. Gives up when denied a requested privilege, item, or activity		Argues, badgers, won't take no for an answer
8. Contemplative, deliberate, not impulsive		Too quick to react, impulsive, engages mouth and muscles before brain		19. Stays on-task despite distractions, focuses, concentrates		Gets off-task, too distracted by noises and people nearby, short attention span
9. Understands why parents/teacher/others are displeased after misbehavior		Feels picked on, is surprised and confused about why others are displeased, doesn't connect own actions to others' reactions		20. Follows through, has an organized approach to activities, finishes projects		Flits from activity to activity, starts things without finishing them, gets sidetracked
10. Plans ahead; thinks about what the results will be before taking action		Careless, doesn't plan ahead; doesn't consider consequences before taking action		21. Doesn't try to bother or hurt others with words		Needles, teases, is mouthy, has to have the last word
11. Cautious about mischief, avoids it		Attracted to or involved in mischief, doesn't distance self from it				

The score is the total number of items in column B plus twice the number of items in column C. The range of possible scores is 0 to 42. An individual (age 2 through adult) scoring 24 or less is probably not hyperactive; 25 to 27: borderline hyperactive; 28 to 32: mildly hyperactive; 33 to 37: moderately hyperactive; 38 to 42: severely hyperactive.

Development and validity data for the original form, which had slightly different wording on some of the items but assessed the same traits on all items, are available from A.D.D. Plus, P.O. Box 4326, Salem, OR 97302.

defiant disorder is particularly troublesome because the child is increasingly at risk for committing acts reflecting a weakened conscience. The next step is conduct disorder, a technical term for juvenile delinquency.

Chemical Repairs

WHEN OPPOSITIONALITY APPEARS as a component of ADHD, it often responds to dietary and pharmaceutical interventions that bring about mood uplift, either through natural nutrients that have an antidepressant action or man-made imitators of those nutrients.

Reducing the oppositionality that is characteristic of ADHD is one of the eight major goals of administering those famous medications—Ritalin is the most prominent—that have aroused so much controversy in recent years.

But there are alternatives to psychotropic drugs: specific foods, nutritional supplements, and insulation from toxic chemicals. A reduction in hyperactivity and inattentiveness is also one of the chief phenomena reported by parents who use the nutritional and toxin insulation approaches to treat ADHD.

> There are alternatives to psychotropic drugs: specific foods, nutritional supplements, and insulation from toxic chemicals.

Brain structure and chemical processes are marvelously complex, and several researchers have high hopes that nutritional studies may hold important keys for unlocking the mysteries of the oppositional child. Until research provides solid answers, we're left simply to speculate about how these chemical interventions interact with the brain to change behavior. Some physicians have theorized that psychotropic drugs stimulate slow-acting neurons and transmitters in the brain. If that theory has any validity, then it's possible, too, that nutritional supplements act in a similar manner, by nourishing malnourished portions of the brain and allowing the brain to synchronize its functions.

Walls Are Built with Bricks of Fear

PHARMACEUTICAL AND DIETARY approaches to helping the ODD child are of limited usefulness unless they are combined with determined efforts to understand and change negative behavior patterns.

Adults who interact with oppositional children—no matter what the origin of the ODD: toxic brain processes, genetics, or life experiences—have to find healthy ways of responding to oppositionality if they are to develop and maintain a positive relationship with the child.

If you picked up this book—or were given it by someone concerned about your child—it's quite likely that you and your child have already reached the point where your interactions have involved some power struggles. You may have relationships with other children who are compliant, gentle, and thoughtful—relationships that have caused you to wonder why it is that your child with ODD is so completely different from "normal" kids.

From a young age, the oppositional child is focused on one thing: power. You may have interpreted that power orientation as being motivated by pride, arrogance, selfishness, or even malice.

It's time for a paradigm shift. Throw out your old, dysfunctional philosophies, theories, laws, and generalizations about why your oppositional child is grasping for power. It's not malice. It's not hatred. Nor is it spite, ill will, or amusement.

The search for power is motivated by fear. Always. Your oppositional child fears your inattention. It might make him "disappear." He fears your disapproval. He wants to "control" you into seeing his perspective. He fears being alone with his own thoughts, for if he sits quietly and contemplates the condition of his life, he might actually have to deal with the guilty, lonely consequences of friendlessness, disapproval, and destructive behaviors. He fears being unloved. In fact, he secretly (or openly) believes that he is unloved.

So he makes sure he's never ignored. Never wrong. Never alone with his quiet thoughts. And never, ever vulnerable to being hurt or unloved.

There is nothing wrong with wanting to feel personal power—everybody does. But a need for an excessive amount of control and power reflects an abnormally high fear of being emotionally vulnerable and—at the same time—an abnormally high craving to feel safe again.

Many years ago, psychologist Abraham Maslow, an influential founder of the humanistic branch of psychology, proposed that the two most basic human needs are physiological needs (air, food, water) and the need for safety—the avoidance of pain and hurt. Maslow's basic assertions have stood the test of time. And they help explain the oppositional child. At his very core, the power-oriented child or teen fears being hurt, and so he works to control everything and everybody who comes near. All refusals to cooperate, refusals to try, and refusals to communicate ultimately reflect fear—the fear of being hurt.

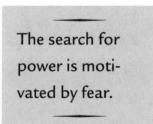

The search for power is motivated by fear.

This fear may or may not have any basis in reality. Young children live in a scary world where big people have the power to feed them, move them about, diaper them, ignore them, spank them, kiss them, or leave them in their crib. Young children are also astonishingly superstitious. They believe their actions "cause" results. If they cry, Mommy comes. If they smile, Mommy smiles. But this "magic" goes much further. If they point their left toe, Mommy might leave. If they sneeze, Mommy turns on the television. If they say "ba," Mommy reads a book. To young children who are trying hard to make connections between causes and effects, it feels as though the world responds or fails to respond based entirely on their own actions.

The downside of this experimenting is that when bad things happen, young children believe they "caused" the bad thing to happen. And sometimes, young children carry this superstition to extremes. "If raising my elbow makes Mommy fight with Daddy, then maybe if I lower my elbow, Mommy and Daddy will stop fighting."

There was once a point in time (perhaps even several) when the hypercontrolling child experienced an unjust "hurt." That child came to believe that if he worked really hard at maintaining control, that hurt would never happen again. The hurt could have been real, but it could just as easily have arisen out of a superstition—a faulty connection between cause and effect. Perhaps one day Mommy didn't notice a hurt knee or hugged a neighbor child or failed to make his favorite kind of sandwich. Perhaps at that moment, the child suffered an emotional "injury" the parent knew nothing about.

Whether genuinely traumatic or easily overlooked, something in that child's past resulted in his believing that if he didn't "control" his world, he'd be hurt. And so he began demanding that Mommy examine every hurt knee very, very closely. Or that Mommy hug only him. Or that Mommy always make the "right" kind of sandwich. In this magical worldview, the fact that things happened exactly as the child expected became proof of infallibility, of safety, of everything being "right" in his sphere. And every disappointment became proof that he wasn't loved or cared for or safe.

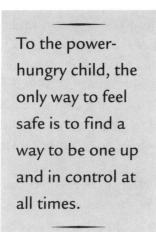

To the power-hungry child, the only way to feel safe is to find a way to be one up and in control at all times.

Rationally, there may no longer be any likelihood of his being traumatized again by the "wrong" sandwich. But superstition isn't rational. Often, the controlling person doesn't even remember the basis of the superstition. It's long buried beneath a pile of self-perpetuating evidence. But the fear of being hurt again drives the child or teen to overcontrol every situation.

To the power-hungry child, the only way to feel safe is to find a way to be one up and in control at all times. Any pressure that makes a child or teen feel more weak or vulnerable will result in renewed attempts at overcontrol.

The Need for Autonomy

BEYOND THE FIRST two needs, every person has two additional basic emotional needs. The first of those higher needs is the need to belong. Being noticed, accepted, appreciated, loved, and treated with respect are all variations on that same need.

The second need, nearly equal in importance, is the need for autonomy. This need manifests itself as a desire to express choice and opinion, to avoid excessive dependency on others, to feel strong and powerful enough to influence the factors that in turn affect him, to have self-confidence, and to feel competent to handle life's demands.

The child or teen who seems to be going through life with an excess need to display personal power has usually not experienced enough healthy autonomy in the first place.

The Importance of a Healthy Contact Boundary

OVER TIME, HUMAN beings develop what we call a "contact boundary." This boundary regulates how much and in what way communication is exchanged between two individuals.

The emotionally healthy individual has a nearly invisible contact boundary with the world that allows that person to have psychological intimacy with loved ones and courteous relationships with acquaintances and strangers. The key is allowing free flow of emotional commerce back and forth across it. Incoming messages are accepted from others, and emotionally relevant messages and actions are sent back across the boundary from the healthy person to the world. An encouraged person with a healthy sense of self has no problem accepting messages from others—including authority figures—and responding to them in a socially appropriate, caring manner. For example, in response to a parent's request, "Please turn down the volume on the television—it's too loud," an encouraged child with a healthy emotional contact boundary would probably lower the volume quickly without so much as a second thought about the incident. The child (1) allows the parent's message to cross his or her contact boundary, (2) accepts the message as a valid request (as opposed to a joke or trick), (3) feels an obligation to respond to the message sender in a cooperative and caring manner, and (4) does so.

But what if the contact boundary is no longer open to the free flow of emotional commerce? The child who fears being hurt by incoming messages will attempt to erect a wall instead—a wall built with bricks of fear.

The porous boundary that should allow a full flow of messages back and forth has become a solid wall that blocks the flow of emotional commerce in both directions. A blocked boundary prevents the child from receiving and accepting messages from outside and undercuts the child's sense of obligation to respond in an emotionally relevant manner. The child's actions no longer mesh with the message sent from others. If anything, they oppose or contradict the incoming message.

In our example, after the parent's request, "Please turn down the volume on the television—it's too loud," the discouraged child who fears being hurt by incoming messages might (1) do nothing at all, thereby indicating total rejection of the parent's message, (2) challenge the validity of the parent's request ("No, it isn't too loud"), (3) attack the message sender ("Mind your own business"), or (4) refuse to send a compliant or helpful action back across the contact boundary ("If you want it lower, do it yourself").

The discouraged child or teen turns what started out as a flexible boundary rich in emotional commerce that travels back and forth across it into a solid wall that prevents the flow of incoming and outgoing messages. Why? What went wrong? Why has the child or teen become convinced that he will become hurt if others' actions and messages are allowed to come to him across the contact boundary or if he sends responsive messages in return?

Previously, I mentioned the early thought processes—the magical thinking—that might cause a child to believe that he has to "control" his world. Another potential root of defiance is that the child simply has not experienced enough autonomy. While the first cause—superstition—originates in faulty

Discovering the Two High-Level Needs

Here is a quick, powerful way to demonstrate the two higher-level needs every child has. I often use this fascinating exercise during my seminars. Most of you won't be conducting seminars, but you can easily do this at home with a spouse, a friend, or your children, or you can picture it in your mind:

1. Ask participants to pair up, become Person A and Person B, and have a 1-minute get-acquainted conversation.

2. After about 60 seconds, tell partners to stand about 8 feet apart, facing each other, with no obstructions between them. Tell A to stand still. Give these instructions to B: "B, keeping your hands to your sides, position yourself at a distance and a closeness from A at which you are more comfortable. Go ahead and move."

3. After 10 seconds, say: "B, return to your original location, please." Then repeat the above instruction, reversing the roles.

4. After 10 seconds, thank the participants and ask them to be seated.

5. Lead a discussion in which you point out that neither was asked to approach, yet both did so. Neither was asked to stand apart from his or her partner, yet both did. Both partners demonstrated a universal need to experience two needs—belonging (moving closer together) and autonomy (staying some distance apart)—rather than merely one or the other.

thinking that needs to be unlearned, in the second—lack of autonomy—defiance might actually be an expected, nearly healthy response to faulty adult behavior. Here are some considerations to examine. Any of these factors might be contributing to your child's oppositional nature.

Unhealthy Handling of Feelings

PERHAPS THE CHILD has discovered that honest communication of personal feelings can be dangerous. If the family, class, or group has an unhealthy style of communicating feelings and wants, the child may not be able to find any alternative to power-oriented misbehavior. Children in these families perceive that their feelings are dishonored, not attended to, or unimportant to parents. If parents or other caregivers talk to them in ways that belittle them or cause them to feel impotent, weak, or one down, they hunt for ways to regain a sense of power and strength. These children operate under the premise of "If I don't watch out for me, who will?" The result is a parade of demands. Chapter 3 provides an extensive discussion of how to create greater emotional safety with children.

Competition Within the Family

IF SIBLING RIVALRY, favoritism, or other forms of competition are encouraged in the home or school, poor winners and poor losers will result. The winners will feel obligated to lord it over their victims, and the losers will be quick to complain. The children might conclude that the only way to survive emotionally is to turn nearly every transaction with others into a win-lose event—an opportunity to defeat someone. They will transform what should be horizontal cooperative relationships into vertical competitive conflicts, with an obsession for being one up over others in nearly every circumstance. Chapter 6 shows how to create a healthy emotional atmosphere among siblings.

A Stressed Emotional History

WHILE IT'S RARELY the optimal response, becoming oppositional can be a relatively healthy reaction to unhealthy parenting, teaching, coaching, or other adult interaction. To understand the roots of oppositionality, examine the child's emotional history. At some point, was this child subjected to negative parenting or other unhealthy interactions with adult caregivers? There are several patterns of maladaptive caregiving that can lead to oppositionality in a child. Some of these patterns involve excessive service toward the child. Others, if carried to their extreme, constitute child abuse.

> If sibling rivalry, favoritism, or other forms of competition are encouraged in the home or school, poor winners and poor losers will result.

Service-Oriented Malparenting

THESE PATTERNS INVOLVE showering the child with exaggerated service and attention. They include taking over the child's life experiences rather than sharing life with the child. Often, in an attempt to compensate for their own feelings of guilt, inadequacy, or neediness, parents become overinvolved in the child's life. There is a great desire to run interference for the child. This overinvolvement manifests itself in several of the following ways:

Overindulgence. Sometimes called spoiling, this form of unhealthy parenting involves excessively shielding the child from frustrations. The parents try to answer every whim and produce a state of constant happiness and contentment for the child, who quickly takes advantage of being treated as "Your Majesty."

Often, these parents felt deprived, underserved, unappreciated, unaccepted, or rejected during their own childhood. Being overindulgent creates a sense of having real impact and of "doing something" for the child. One mother whom I was counseling summarized the guideline by which she had been interacting with her chronically disabled child: "You just breathe; I'll do all the rest for you!"

Overindulgent parents provide too little structure and too few guidelines. Children have a natural desire to expand their talents and push for as much influence as they can have in whatever situation they are in. Like gas that expands to fill the room into which it is released, children will push outward until they find a solid boundary. The apparent absence of any limits will send them on an unending project of limit testing.

Sometimes, children even become disgusted at their parents' lack of limit setting and criticize their parents for being too lax.

A healthy response by the child to this style of unhealthy parenting is to create distance from the oversolicitous parents. One way to create distance is to avoid asking for input. The child can seem oppositional by virtue of being independent and doing things "her way" without consulting her parents about their wishes. Oppositionality can develop also from being given too much authority and becoming power drunk.

Overprotection. If parents are overly watchful for dangers, they can provide excessive shielding from risks and dangers. Their nagging fear is that something bad might happen to the children. The parent says, "Don't climb the ladder; you might fall off. Don't go outside; you might catch a cold. Don't pet the dog; you might get bitten." Deprived of opportunities to develop competence and demonstrate personal power, the children become oppositional in their attempts to experience life more fully. As if to demonstrate disgust with the parents' excessive fearfulness, they seek opportunities to take risks and find adventure with a devil-may-care bravado.

Hypervigilance. A variant of overprotection, this form of unhealthy parenting involves preoccupation with the children's whereabouts, welfare, and activities. The parents are in a constant state of alert, becoming agitated and concerned whenever the children are out of visual or hearing range. They must know everything the children are doing at all times. Parents of busy, energetic, exploratory toddlers or older hyperactive children often sink into this form of service-oriented malparenting.

Often, the parents have a desire to be in control and to supervise in order to be assured of the children's safety and success. This pattern can also stem from an unusual need in the parents to overcontrol and dominate, perhaps out of a fear that the children will rebel against them or abandon them in some way. Similar to a dictator who sends out secret police to hunt for anyone who might be planning a rebellion, the parents overcontrol and in the process must be extra vigilant.

The healthy response by children is to resist the intrusions and constant invasion of privacy. The children try to defend personal boundaries. Often, however, their attempts fail, resulting in the parents increasing their relentless vigil. A stable but unhealthy pattern settles in. The children become resentful but resigned to the parents' hypervigilance; at the same time, the parents resent the children's objections.

Nagging. This pattern is the most common parental error. The parents don't trust the child's ability to pursue goals, handle responsibilities, or do just about anything independently. They give an endless stream of directives, reminders, commands, close supervision, advice, and instructions.

> Nagging is the most common parental error. The parents don't trust the child's ability to pursue goals, handle responsibilities, or do anything independently.

Words are like automobile tires. The more times a tire goes around, the more tread it loses, and the less efficient it becomes at starting, stopping, and steering. The same is true with words used to start, stop, and steer children. The more they are used, the less efficient they become.

Sometimes, the parents are trying to experience great power as compensation for inner feelings of not having been listened to, responded to, or taken seriously during their own childhood. Their goal is to control the situation by forcing the children to comply.

Are You Committing the Number One Parenting Error?

I have developed a handy way to tell whether nagging is a consistent pattern in any parent-child relationship. I call it finding the C & D percent. Here's what to ask:

"Of all the messages you give your child, what percentage is corrective and directive in nature (add both together)?"

CORRECTIVE: scold, criticize, punish, time-out, raised voice

DIRECTIVE: boss, nag, remind, request, order

If the answer is 50 percent or higher, intervention is needed. The ideal figure is 25 percent, and even that should consist largely of calm, polite requests and very few confrontations.

Sometimes, the source of this pattern is external to the parents, such as when raising a hyperactive child. The parents might feel trapped into nagging: "If I don't nag him about it, he'll never do what he's supposed to do."

The children who resist this form of parenting might set up power struggles and refuse to comply. The escalation looks like this: The parent raises her voice and floods the child with orders and threats, to which the child responds, "Go ahead and punish me. See if I care!" Passive-resistant and passive-aggressive behavior such as dawdling and sneaking behind parents' backs might also develop. Or the child might simply make direct appeals such as "Leave me alone!" or "Stop bugging me!" All of these forms of resistance could be interpreted as being oppositional in nature.

Exploitation-Oriented Malparenting

ANY FORM OF child abuse represents a vicious assault on personal boundaries, initiating what for many abuse victims will become for them a lifetime of overconcern about the emotional contact boundary. Not all instances of parents' raised voices, critical comments, spanking, and the like constitute abuse. Generally speaking, these patterns cross over the line when they are nonaccidental, frequent, or severe, or when they violate reasonable standards of decency and courtesy and have a destructive effect on the child.

Abusive parents are generally of two types. They either have normal psychological strength but have been stretched beyond their limits of coping or have severe character flaws or psychiatric problems.

The ability to cope with life's stresses is a reflection of an individual's overall level of mental health. Diagnosable psychiatric conditions can impact a parent's capacity to absorb the stress associated with child rearing. If children are particularly difficult to deal with, an us-against-them attitude can develop between parents and their children. Parents with a history of significant substance abuse, criminal tendencies, paranoid or psychotic conditions, or similar profound disturbances are more at risk for committing child abuse whenever parenting responsibilities become especially demanding.

Mentally healthy parents generally resort to child abuse only under severely stressful circumstances. They might feel completely defeated by a child's defiance. Chronic opposition might eventually lead to unconquerable anger toward the child. They might be overwhelmed by the years of trying to juggle the nonstop demands of their oppositional teenager. They might be caught in a double-bind situation, where keeping the child or teen satisfied means that the needs of other family members go unmet. There is a certain desperation that occurs within the parent who steps over the line into the abuse level of malparenting.

Exploitative malparenting that can cause a child to develop excessive oppositionality reflects a state of emotional exhaustion in the parents. Parents who are otherwise psychologically healthy feel guilty after they let loose on an oppositional child. They might make perfectionistic vows such as "Today I will be calm and loving." Indications of the end-of-rope state include weakened levels of patience, tolerance, and emotional control. When at this stage, parents are declaring emotional bankruptcy. Yelling and screaming might, in fact, seem like the most humane way to deal with an impossible situation. Some parents excuse this pattern with rationalizations such as "If I weren't yelling at him, I'd be hitting him" and "I'm just a yeller."

Another sign of emotional bankruptcy is parents' sense of defeat and a low amount of positive or loving communication toward the child or teen. The percentage of messages that are critical or disciplinary (the C & D percent figure) becomes high—often over 50 percent of the messages sent from the parents to the child.

When nagging doesn't work, the parents might stop trying to exert influence on the child in a "What's the use!" attitude. The parents run out of options and might start hating each day as it starts. Meanwhile, their resentment of the child builds.

Verbal abuse. Verbal abuse represents a verbal version of what would otherwise be a physical beating of the child. The verbally abusive parent regularly belittles and criticizes the child in excess of the flow of corrective messages customarily occurring from most supervising adults to the children under their charge. Examples include insults, ridicule, name-calling, yelling, swearing, sarcasm, and the use of profanity.

There is another element to verbal abuse. The parent is trying to push the child down through criticism and belittlement. This pattern can also reflect a need in parents to feel personally elevated over the child. Often, verbally abusive parents were themselves verbally abused as children and at last have a safe, familiar opportunity for getting revenge and being one up.

To fight back, a child might display anger and determination to defend personal boundaries with a statement such as "Keep your criticisms to yourself!" or other evidences of oppositionality. Because the parent is using the verbal channel of communication so heavily, the child has an automatic invitation to use the same channel. Verbal power struggles—shouting matches—are the result.

Physical abuse. This form of unhealthy parenting involves hitting, slapping, strapping, kicking, throwing, shaking, burning, hair pulling, biting, spraying, excessive twirling or tickling, excessive spanking, or other forms of assault. More extreme forms border on or actually constitute torture.

The most common forms of physical abuse occur with parents who feel they are at the end of their rope. The intention is to "teach a lesson." Unfortunately, the only lessons the child learns are that the world is unsafe and that the child is unloved. Interestingly, when confronted, these parents tend to self-righteously defend their version of "punishment" as legitimate discipline. Any attempt at stopping their pattern of abuse usually amounts to little more than "ritualizing" the hitting by putting arbitrary limits on it. For many reasons, I strongly advise against a punishment-oriented discipline style for raising children who are externalizers, such as those who are hyperactive or oppositional.

Physically abusive parents—like their verbal counterparts—often were abused as children. They may be venting pent-up feelings of revenge toward their own abusers from long ago. The child is an easy target, especially if disobedient or difficult to manage. Hyperactive children are overrepresented as victims of this as well as all other forms of child abuse. Many children and teens with oppositional defiant disorder are also hyperactive. Interestingly, many abusive parents are hyperactive adults. There is recent research evidence that their abusive tendencies are a reflection of their impatience and impulsiveness. They are excessive and impulsive, rather than sneaky and conniving, in their abusive discipline of their children.

> The most common forms of physical abuse occur with parents who feel they are at the end of their rope. The intention is to "teach a lesson."

The child who resists by reaching out beyond the family to friends, social agencies, or school personnel often is greeted with disbelief by adults who want to minimize or deny the existence of the abuse. There is almost no middle ground for the child, who concludes that the only viable options are putting up with being abused, running away, counterattacking the parents, or committing suicide. The oppositionality would then appear in the form of running away and wanting to avoid submitting to the parents in any form.

Child neglect. Withholding ordinary care and services requires the child to perform alone the daily activities typically regarded as part of the protective and guiding duties of parents. Protective duties include providing shelter, clothing, food, medical care, and related services of physical needs. Guiding functions include paying attention to the child's needs and wants, talking with the child, and arranging for the child to participate in normal social and educational functions.

Brief periods of neglect can occur when end-of-rope parents have given up struggling to serve the child. In more pathological families, the parents neglect the child as a reflection of global immaturities and inability to assume responsibilities. Parents with a psychosis and those with severe character disorders or patterns of substance abuse are most likely to commit this form of child abuse. They want to focus all their coping energy on fulfilling their own needs so that there is none left over with which to cope with the child. Neglectful parents often appear to be inefficient employees and sloppy homemakers who spend a considerable amount of time engaging in frivolous and passive entertainment. They tend to be poor at setting and attaining long-term goals, instead being impulsive in nature.

Children who resist learn to function autonomously at too young an age and in too many areas. The result is a miniature adult who is very assertive and might appear oppositional.

Emotional abuse. This form of unhealthy parenting involves not permitting the child to feel loved. The parents' actions can include harassing, taunting, rejecting, confusing, belittling, demeaning, incorrectly accusing, depriving of basic emotional needs, sending repeated messages of disgust and disappointment, voicing perfectionistic expectations toward the child, and exploiting the child. Their intention is to cause and observe confusion and suffering in the child. Examples include refusing to do any favors for the child, avoiding affectionate touching or contact, not providing gifts when gift giving is called for, overreacting to the child's actions on some occasions while giving very little reaction on other identical occasions, and conveying strong "I hate you" messages.

They tend to dwell on the child's shortcomings and alleged weaknesses, compare the child unfavorably with other children, or by various other statements and actions undermine the child's sense of worth and emotional safety. Giving children simultaneous "come here–go away" messages is a form of emotional abuse. For example, a parent tricks the child into coming close, then turns on the child with an "I hate you" message or some sort of physical assault. The frontal attack on the child's self-esteem has devastating consequences for the victim of this form of abuse.

Being unaccepting of the child and showing a perfectionistic demand for adult-level performance and judgment can also reflect emotional abuse. Rigid, demanding, perfectionistic, materialistic parents who are at the end-of-rope state emotionally are at risk for committing this form of child abuse. Often, these parents have serious psychiatric conditions such as substance abuse, character disorders, paranoid conditions, or psychotic disturbances. Usually, emotionally abusive parents have trouble bonding, with a history of unstable intimate relationships. They usually are not very capable of experiencing true love for another person. Sometimes, these parents are rather inept at most interpersonal skills.

> Giving children simultaneous "come here–go away" messages is a form of emotional abuse.

The best defense against the emotional torture of being blatantly unloved is to avoid seeking after the impossible goal of being loved. Accordingly, the children try to develop the protective maneuver of distancing from the parents and discontinuing efforts to please them. They pursue the opposite goal of regarding the parents' stamp of approval with disdain, and they find ways to express disgust toward the parents. They also erect barriers to weaken the parent-child bonds. They go places without asking, make decisions without seeking parents' advice, and generally try to become as autonomous and self-sufficient as possible. Again, we find apparent oppositionality occurring as a healthy response to pathological parenting.

Dejuvenilizing. Also known as mutual dependency, symbiotic dependency, and adultification, this form of unhealthy parenting is actually a variant of emotional abuse. Parents treat their children as substitutes for adults in trying to obtain closeness, companionship, and emotional intimacy. They use children to meet emotional needs that should normally be met through their relationships with other adults. The children become their crying towels, advice givers, companions, and confidantes.

When parents want advice about adult-level issues, they put heavy pressure for key decision making onto the children. A role reversal sets in, and the children take on adult-level emotional leadership while the parents become increasingly dependent on emotional support from the children. The parents actually carry on adult-level emotional commerce with the children. They become emotional offspring, and the children become emotional parents.

Usually, these parents have felt lonely or unsupported in childhood as well as adulthood. Unable to find appropriate adults for intimacy processes, they exploit their children. Sexual abuse of children is a variant of this type of abuse.

Meanwhile, the children lose the benefit of normal, healthy protections against emotional stress. Their stress umbrellas (discussed in chapter 3) are very leaky. Serious emotional overburdening is likely to occur.

They might try valiantly to fulfill these gigantic expectations. Having essentially lost the services of mature parenting to assist in going through life, they learn to avoid asking others for help with anything. An unfortunate lesson often learned in this situation is that the world isn't a safe or nurturing place.

The children develop a "look out for myself" self-centeredness as a survival tactic because there literally is nobody else available to help look out for their needs.

The healthiest response is to create emotional distance in order to provide some safety and insulation against the parents' intrusions. The children avoid coming home and try to become enmeshed in peer relationships or relationships with healthy role models outside the family. Meanwhile, they develop ever-increasing disgust for their immature, incompetent parents.

Children who resist the role of surrogate parent must try to set realistic personal boundaries, often at great cost in terms of generating conflict with the parents. The parents might use "If you really loved me" ploys to get the children to stay in the role of surrogate parent. The children will resist, however, using name-calling, angry displays, open defiance, sneaking out and leaving the parents alone, and other means. All of these resistances are quite oppositional in nature.

It is important to understand the roots of oppositionality. I am delighted to provide hundreds of high-impact methods to relieve the situation throughout the pages of this book, but no book can substitute for skilled professional counseling. If the child is reflecting any of the victimizations discussed in this chapter, seek appropriate help.

The next chapter discusses the ways in which an oppositional child or teen will tend to display his or her excess need for power and control.

2

How Your Child Displays Power

PROBLEMS IN EXPRESSING emotions lead to oppositional defiant misbehavior. One of the most marvelous aspects of children is their ability to express their emotions. This
trait should be cherished and nurtured. From the moment of
their birth, children have ways of directly expressing their desires to have their needs met. All children start out as expert
communicators of their needs. Their facial expressions, cries,
and body movements provide clear indication that they are experiencing hunger or discomfort on the one hand and contentment and pleasure on the other.

Beyond infancy, children continue expressing emotional
needs in a clear and direct manner. The technical name for this
process is *emotional congruence.* Just as two triangles are said to
be congruent if they are perfect copies of each other, children's
body talk and actions are congruent if they reflect the children's genuine feelings and needs. Congruence is healthy;

31

incongruence is not. The goal is to get your child to stay congruent and to encourage congruent communication among all family members. Chapter 3 discusses this concept in detail.

There are two basic reasons why children don't express their emotional needs congruently to parents: It is not safe to do so, or it is not profitable. Children who don't feel safe to assert emotional needs fear that they will receive abuse, criticism, or rejection from the parent or another adult. Those who are listened to but for whom the adult doesn't take cooperative action soon give up trying to get needs met through polite expression.

> The two basic reasons children don't express their emotional needs to parents: It is not safe to do so, or it is not profitable.

Suppose, for example, that a child lives with a verbally and emotionally abusive parent who is also an alcoholic. The child's predominant need and fervent hope is that the parent will stop the abusive behavior that occurs during the states of drunkenness. So the child gets up enough nerve to ask the parent to stop drinking. The parent reacts with an explosive rage, and the child immediately learns never again to express that wish out loud because to do so isn't safe.

But what if the parent doesn't react with a tantrum but instead listens with apparent attention and respect for the child's wishes? The child is elated. Two days later, the parent victimizes the child with yet another state of drunken verbal abusiveness. The child gradually learns that, while it is safe to express this feeling and desire, it isn't profitable. Nothing changed from attempting to assert personal wants toward the parent.

Children usually start out with congruent, direct statements but learn to take incongruent detours when direct and honest expression seems unsafe or unprofitable. Once the channels for correct expression are cut off, children tend to display their feelings through misbehavior and oppositional defiance.

Three Basic Messages

POWER-ORIENTED CHILDREN and teens usually have given up trying to communicate needs congruently. Once they surrender their mutual interaction with caring adults, however, another tragedy unfolds. They begin to falter in conscience development. Conscience is awareness of and concern about one's physical and emotional impact on other people and their feelings. By insisting on what they want, power-displaying children automatically cut off some concern about what the other person wants or needs.

Like all forms of misbehavior, an excessive demand for power reflects an inadequate conscience. Oppositional children and teens give out three basic messages to the world in general and to authority figures and peers in particular. Each message can be reflected in a simple motto:

1. I will control my world: "I want what I want when I want it!"

2. I will control you: "I'm the boss!"

3. I won't let you control me: "You can't make me!"

Oppositional children might be sending one, two, or all three of these messages through their actions and statements.

Patterns of Misbehavior

THERE ARE AT least six common patterns of misbehavior among power-oriented children and teens. The first three primarily involve relationships with peers, while the second three involve relationships with adults. All reflect one or more of the guiding mottoes. They also involve insufficient conscience and compensate for inadequate personal autonomy.

Each of these six major ways for a child to experience power can be aggravated by incorrect parenting actions. This process is called *enabling*. They can also be counteracted by effective strategies. Chapter 6 provides detailed methods for lifting a child out of these patterns.

The Competitor. The Competitor tries to make sure his weaknesses are never revealed. One way is to oppose, defeat, and compete with just about everyone. His goal is to end up on top in nearly every situation. He will inject a win-lose perspective into even the most docile and cooperative of contacts with others. He might point out, for example, that he completed his work before another student did. Or he might make sure that another student notices that the grade he received on his paper is higher than the grade received by his classmate. He tends to be a poor sport who cheats to win, gloats when he triumphs, and complains about the officiating when he loses.

Healthy peer relationships emphasize equality and fairness in terms of how each person treats the other. Such relationships are said to be horizontal in their distribution of power. Decisions are made jointly by taking into account everyone's opinions. A controlling child injects a vertical element that disrupts the normal pattern and sets in motion a chain reaction of unhealthy processes. Competition is—by its very nature—a vertical process. It creates a one-up/one-down relationship between peers. The Competitor must be "better than" and must, of course, always be a winner. Therefore, there must always also be a loser: "I must win, so you must lose."

Parenting actions that enable this pattern can include upholding competition as desirable. Many parents mistakenly believe they are doing their children a service by honing their children's competitive skills. Competition, however, is not a healthy process to inject into a classroom or a family. Comparing the child with others, including siblings, is another dangerous parenting error. Competition and direct comparison destroy love and chew away at conscience. Parents who set an example of comparing themselves with others or who make judgmental statements and evaluations of others magnify this type of power display.

The Show-Off. The Show-Off goes out of her way to prove how superior she is to others and does so with a sanctimonious or moralistic twist. This type of power display represents a vindictive form of arrogance. A put-down artist, she will comment that her handwriting is more graceful than another student's, that she turned in her paper sooner, that she is a better dresser, or even that she is more humble than the other person!

> Healthy peer relationships emphasize equality and fairness in terms of how each person treats the other.

Like all put-down artists, this child's real wish is to feel elevated in compensation for secret feelings of weakness and inferiority. Ironically, feeding into either the child's arrogance or her underlying feelings of inferiority will magnify this type of power display. Telling her that she is doing well, for example, will not stop her desire to show off but will expand it. Telling her the opposite message—that she has not done well—will also push her into renewed attempts to compensate for her presumed inferiority by showing off.

Thus both praise and criticism in and of themselves lead to escalation of this particular power display. Parents who act arrogant about their own accomplishments or talents make this type of problem worse.

The Boss. The Boss obtains power the easy way—by grabbing it quickly before anyone else does. He will simply assume command and start ordering others around. This quick action puts him in a one-up position over his peers. He is ready to defend his newfound power against anyone who dares to challenge him for domination of the event or circumstance. Hes will often select playmates who are weak, underassertive, or many years younger. Sometimes, the boss is driven by a morbid fear of the entire emotional environment. The only way to be safe is to control everyone as completely as possible. The Boss may seem to give orders in a frantic, indiscriminate style and may become visibly upset if others choose to act independently.

One way parents can accidentally train a child into this pattern is by surrendering too much of their authority and allowing the child to have too much say in things. This enabling action affirms the child's apparent right to dictate to others. While it is important to let children have a sense of influence over their destinies, parents can create a power-drunk child if they overshoot the mark. There is an ideal balance point between letting a child have influence and letting him rule the roost.

The Debater. Debaters are argumentative. They have to have the last word—or the last gesture as they leave—in every conversation. Stubborn, unwilling to compromise, and masters of "Yes, but . . . ," they can transform any conversation into an argument. The verbal power play is the great equalizer. As long as the weapons for the conflict are words, these children can be a match for any adult willing to accept an invitation to debate. If children and teens can keep adults in a verbal power struggle—nagging, arguing, debating—they are at least equal to the adult who engages them.

Children are often trained into using this pattern by parents who use the verbal channel too much. Effective parenting

Dealing with the Debater

Alex was old enough to help with household chores but persuading him to pitch in was almost impossible. "Alex, could you pick up those clothes and put them in the hamper?" his mother would ask. "They're not dirty," Alex would respond. "Yes they are." "They are not." No matter what his parents asked, Alex had an argument: "I already did it." "I have to do all the work around here." And the most annoying of all: "Why?" For years, Alex's parents debated with him. They would patiently try to explain why a particular chore needed to be done, but their explanations were never sufficient. Instead, Alex perceived the explanation as an invitation to argue. When his parents finally started screaming, Alex would sulk and do the chore so slowly that his frustrated parents would just send him to his room—playland—and do the chore themselves.

Eventually, they stumbled on a better solution. One day Alex's mother asked him to empty the wastebaskets. He attempted to debate. This attempt was met with "I would like you to empty the waste baskets. Please do so now." When he demanded an explanation, she found herself still calm, and simply announced a consequence: "If I have to repeat myself, or if you sulk or argue, there will be no lunch." She then went back to her own work and walked away from the debate. Much to her amazement, Alex emptied the wastebasket—cheerfully!

isn't necessarily highly verbal. In fact, calm leadership often involves saying relatively little and letting actions do the talking. Explaining and justifying everything to excess will simply train the child to become a Debater. Listening for too long to a child's rambling complaints is also an error. These children often have considerable experience luring their parents into long verbal power struggles, during which they hone their debating skills and gain an increased sense of arrogance and power. Probably the ideal mechanism for getting away with being oppositional, debate improves the odds of wearing adults down and getting one's own way.

The Sneak. Sometimes, a child learns to become very distrustful of what adults say and what they want. The safest option for these children is to appear to be compliant while they plot to do the opposite of whatever the adult says. The sneak will use passive-aggressive and surreptitious means to get what she wants when she wants it. She will become adept at misbehaving behind the backs of parents and teachers. She will do whatever she wants to do, with no regard for rules, and she will try to keep it a secret from the authority figures for as long as possible. Afterward, if the adults find out what she did, she can become a debater and argue about how she was justified in her actions and about how unfair the adults are.

Enabling responses from parents include affirming the child's power to disobey adult authority. Parents might tell the child that she can veto what they say or that others (which, by extension, includes themselves) have no right to influence what she does. Another common enabling response is to overstate faith and confidence in the child's judgment, as when parents comment favorably on or chuckle about how strong-willed, determined, stubborn, or bullheaded the child can be. The child happily conforms to the parents' apparent endorsements.

The Rebel. One step up from the debater in intensity is the even more stubborn, uncompromising, and openly defiant rebel who refuses to cooperate and who invites adults to lock horns in a power struggle. Unlike the Sneak, whose quest for power is often hidden from view, the Rebel makes a public spectacle of his power. Openly defiant of legitimate authority, he invites, tricks, or dares the adult into a shouting match or some other blatant head-to-head clash. As with the debater, the real joy occurs during the act of conducting the struggle; just rocking the boat is enough of a victory. Even if the parent rules in the end, the power struggler has felt quite strong and powerful by being involved in a mini war.

> Unlike the sneak, whose quest for power is often hidden from view, the power struggler makes a public spectacle of his power.

Parents enable the Rebel by getting lured into the struggle. If you're in it, you lose. What the child wants is to experience strength by opposing the parent. If the parent even enters the contest, the child gains what he was searching for—a sense of

The Joy of Power Struggling

Here is an entertaining and convincing way to convey an important and often misunderstood aspect of power struggles. You need a baseball bat as a prop. Hold the bat vertically and ask a volunteer to assist you in deciding who is going to bat first. Grasp the bat by wrapping your hand around it near the bottom and saying "Me first!" Coax as needed to get the volunteer to grasp immediately above your hand and say the same line, "Me first!" Repeat this sequence until one of you caps the top of the bat.

Explain to the group that you didn't care who capped the bat. Several times during this exchange, your hand was above the competitor's hand. You got your kicks by having several "little victories" during the course of the power struggle. In the same way, a power-struggling child automatically experiences strength and power by virtue of being in the struggle, not necessarily by "winning" the struggle.

great interpersonal power without having to conform to the needs of the situation or of others. In the midst of a power struggle, it's hard to tell who is the parent and who is the child.

Conscience Problems

ONCE YOU PERCEIVE power-oriented misbehavior as an indication of inadequate conscience, it becomes more understandable. Many of the traits of people who have an underdeveloped conscience also occur in children and teens who seek excess experiencing of power.

Here are several common behavior patterns of power-oriented children and teens that reflect inadequate conscience. Just as with the six patterns of power display, it is important to recognize when these behavior patterns are occurring so you can counteract them or stop them from escalating.

Lying. Purposely omitting or distorting the truth can serve several aims in a power play. By creating mental chaos and sending the listener in wrong directions, lying puts children in a one-up position and makes the listener more vulnerable. Lying is most commonly used by the Sneak, the Debater, and the Show-Off. The claims of these three types of power-displaying children are the least verifiable, so they can more often get away with deceptiveness.

There are three categories of lies: claims to be "more than" the reality, claims to be "less than" the reality, and claims to be "other than" the reality. In addition, there are three types of lies within each category.

"More than" claims. Claims to be more than they are involve arrogance, grandiosity, and inflated portrayals of the child's accomplishments. Here are the three types:

- **Claims of commission.** These claims are usually made to gain favor or impress someone. The child claims to have done things that she actually did not do. "I cleaned my room and did all my chores *on time*."

- **Claims of assent.** These claims are an attempt to avoid displeasing someone or to keep someone from further exploring the issue. The child claims to have a belief or awareness that he actually doesn't have. These claims include those famous "white lies." "Don't worry so much. My room's clean."

- **Claims of exaggeration.** These claims are often an attempt to impress someone or gain extra attention. The child claims to have done things in an amount or to a level more than was actually done. "I *always* keep my room clean."

"Less than" claims. Claims to be less than the reality usually are attempts to appear helpless and innocent in order to dodge responsibility of some sort:

- **Claims of omission.** The opposite of the claim of commission lie, this lie is of the "I didn't do it" variety. It is often given in an attempt to avoid getting caught in or punished for a misdeed. "I didn't make the mess in my room."

- **Claims of forgetting.** The universal ticket out of responsibility is to rely on the very human trait of forgetfulness as the excuse. "I forgot that I was supposed to clean my room."

- **Claims of unawareness.** Even more forgivable than being forgetful is the apparent helplessness of not knowing what was expected in the first place. The charm of innocence is hard to resist. "I didn't know you wanted me to clean my room."

"Other than" claims. Claims that the event is the fault and responsibility of other persons or external forces are additional ways to dodge responsibility:

- **Blaming other people.** Pointing the accusing finger away from themselves and toward others is a handy ticket out from feeling responsible. "You left the keys out, so I thought I could take the car."

- **Blaming circumstances, nature, and animals.** Events that are uncontrollable, such as the weather or the unpredictable actions of animals, make for easy excuses to avoid responsibility. "The dog destroyed my homework." "I forgot because it was raining."

- **Minimizing and excusing.** Some lies displace responsibility altogether. "I know a lot of kids who shoplift in this store." "I thought it was a free sample."

All of these forms of lying have social purposes and reinforce the child's power in the situation. Almost all lying is a power play of some sort, so it's right in line with the typical behavior of oppositional children and teens.

Impatience. A reliable general indicator of emotional immaturity, impatience is reflected in tendencies to seek only immediate gratification. Living primarily for pleasure in the here and now, sometimes called *short-term hedonism*, is the hallmark of emotionally immature individuals of any age.

An "I want what I want when I want it" attitude often accompanies oppositional behavior. The impatient child will try to do things the easy way rather than the more diligent way. She will be quick to give up and move on to a less challenging circumstance or set of responsibilities. The impatient child or teen tends to act upon the first impulse, no matter what the consequence. There is often a tendency to expect gratification without paying the price in terms of time and effort. After all, diligent and responsible actions are not pleasurable.

Impatience and impulsiveness go hand in hand. The impatient child or teen seldom displays interest in activities that

> Almost all lying is a power play of some sort, so it's right in line with the typical behavior of oppositional children and teens.

develop self-mastery or involve significant self-restraint and self-discipline. In fact, some authorities now regard conduct disorder as a combination of impatience, impulsiveness, and hostility.

Hostility. Hostile actions involve a predatory, destructive approach toward other people. These actions indicate emotional immaturity and are strong signs of insufficient conscience development. Hostility can be reflected in words or actions, but with power-oriented children and teens, it usually is indicated verbally rather than by overt attacks on people or animals.

Language choice often reflects powerfully hostile emotions. The typical child or teen is subjected to tens of thousands of profanities and obscenities through the media, peers, and contact with adults. It's nearly impossible to shield a child or teen from hearing offensive, profane, or obscene uses of language. Nevertheless, children who don't show hostility, defiance, or other dysfunctions seem to have little trouble controlling their language. I have noted that children and teens who pepper their verbal expressions with profanities generally tend to have a great amount of built-up hostility. A foul mouth usually indicates a cesspool of rancid, built-up anger and resentment.

Sassing, talking back, and speaking disrespectfully to or about authority figures are both discourteous and hostile. Similarly, the elderly, the very young, the weak, the mistaken, the disabled, and other people in vulnerable positions make easy targets for ridicule, put-downs, and other forms of verbal attack. Purposefully being a pest and going out of the way to annoy others is another reflection that the child or teen is burdened with built-up hostility.

Irritability. Closely related to hostility, irritability also reflects built-up resentment. Both irritability and hostility represent abnormal handling of anger. Anger is a healthy emotional mechanism for self-protection. It gives us the ability to become energized and focused when we perceive our needs to be under threat. Whereas hostility reflects an abnormal *amount* of anger, irritability represents an abnormally weak *lid* on anger. This child or teen is thin-skinned, easily offended or upset, with a low tolerance for frustration. This state is commonly known as having a "short fuse." The amount of anger displayed during moments of irritability can vary from making a fist to exploding in rage.

> Closely related to hostility, irritability also reflects built-up resentment.

Anger is a secondary, self-protective, energizing, focusing, emotional response to a primary hurt or the possibility of being hurt in some way. It is a secondary response because—unlike the first and primary experience of being hurt—anger is only one of several possible subsequent responses to a given provocation. For example, if you were to hit your thumb with a hammer, your initial response would be a combination of pain and surprise. Your secondary response is a choice: You could shout, curse, take deep breaths, laugh, get angry, get indignant, criticize yourself, or hop up and down.

There is a connection between being a hyperactive person and having severe anger control problems. Anger is one of the chief characteristics of children who have attention deficit hyperactivity disorder (ADHD). I have found in my extensive work in the field of ADHD that the majority of hyperactive children and teens have some sort of significant anger control problem that interferes with their adjustment. Anger responds well to all three physiological treatment approaches for ADHD: prescribed medications, nutrition, and insulation from toxic chemical exposure. The majority of adults with

What Are You Mad At?

Here is a powerful little story to teach the important lesson that anger is a secondary reaction to a primary hurt. It is based on our interpretation of a perceived hurt, not on the hurt itself.

Tell this story to a group, couple, or individual. "You and a companion are standing next to each other on the sidewalk. A man comes by, steps on your foot, then on your companion's foot, and walks away. You are outraged, but your companion smiles at you calmly. 'How can you be so calm after what that man just did to us?' you ask, ready to explode. Your companion answers: 'Didn't you notice? That man is blind.'"

Discuss the story's meaning. What happened to your anger? You and your friend were both equally stepped on. Is anger based on the fact of being stepped on, or is it based on your interpretation of that event?

severe anger control problems probably have the adult form of ADHD. Clearly there are numerous tie-ins between impulsivity, impatience, muscle activity, and anger.

Nearly everyone gets angry now and then. The level of irritability to be concerned about is one in which the child or teen is being disrupted—and is disruptive to others—beyond a frequency to be expected from normal day-to-day stresses. People who can't "control their temper" are giving evidence of a breakdown of normal self-control mechanisms. I consider problems in anger control to be a sign of insufficient conscience development.

Self-centeredness. Selfishness, or egocentrism, is a distorted form of self-care that involves enhancing oneself at the expense of others. A "What's in it for me?" attitude leaves little room to care about the welfare or happiness of the other person. Self-centeredness is commonly observed among people who don't have a fully developed conscience, because conscience by its very definition involves concern about impact on others. Self-centeredness in power-oriented, misbehaving children can appear as part of the impatience trait discussed above. Self-centeredness manifests itself as a seeming lack of caring about the effects of behavior on others and an inability to empathize with the hurt they cause with their misbehavior.

> The use of addictive substances by a child or teen should always be taken as a sign of serious emotional problems.

Substance abuse. The use of addictive substances by a child or teen should always be taken as a sign of serious emotional problems, at least to the extent of bringing the matter to the attention of a skilled helping professional. The bottom line is that addictive substances numb the person against feeling life's pain. But why the need for that extent of numbing? Usually, there are significant things going wrong in the child's life that are generating more emotional pain than he can cope with.

Externalizing. Part of the arrogance of oppositional and defiant children and teens is their tendency to shove blame off of themselves and onto others. Externalizing blame and responsibility allows children to escape the pain of acknowledging the damage they cause. Conscience involves being concerned about your impact on others. When a teenager externalizes, however, he needn't feel guilty about lying to his

Is Your Child Sneaking Drugs?

Here are warning signs of drug use in teens. Watch for bizarre, extreme, dramatic changes; some could be rapid, others could be gradual. Seek appropriate professional help if you notice any of these signs:

Changes in Behavior
- Dreamy, blank expression
- Stupor, drowsiness
- Shakiness
- Lack of coordination
- Slurred speech
- Incoherent speech
- Rapid, meandering speech
- Needle marks
- Bloodstains on sleeves
- Discolored fingers
- Dry mouth
- Watery, bloodshot eyes; enlarged eye pupils
- Runny nose
- Excessive itching
- Marked appetite increase
- No appetite
- Marked sweets craving
- Vomiting
- Strong body odor
- Uncontrolled laughing, silliness
- Uncontrolled crying, sadness
- Marked aggressiveness
- Extreme fatigue
- Chain-smoking

parents because, for instance, failing to do household chores can be blamed on parents who didn't write it down correctly on the note on the refrigerator. There is no need to feel guilty about causing pain to a teacher by being rude because the teacher deserved it.

Discoveries in Your Home

- Large paper bags
- Large handkerchiefs
- Tubes of glue, glue smears
- Needles, syringes
- Cotton balls
- Tourniquet supplies (string, rope)
- Bottle caps, spoons
- Strange burning odors
- Cigarette paper
- Sugar cubes (especially if discolored)
- Small tubes for liquids
- Jars with pills or capsules
- Pills or capsules of suspicious origin

Changes in Your Teen's Behavior and Habits

- Rapid disappearance of clothing and personal belongings because the teen is selling them for drugs
- Unusual activity around hangouts, under large bridges, mall parking lots, hallways frequented by addicts and pushers
- Spending unusual amounts of time in bedroom or bathroom with the door locked
- Inability to hold down a job or stay in school
- Rejection of or from old friends; taking up with suspicious new companions
- Using jargon that addicts use

Externalizing allows the child to take a one-up position in every circumstance. It also provides a way to maintain arrogance and numbness about the impact of his actions. It works against the development of conscience. Criminals usually are very adept at externalizing. When asked why they are in prison, their first responses typically involve blaming the police, courts, victims, witnesses, politicians, or relatives.

Irresponsibility. There is great power in appearing unable or unwilling to perform for adults. Avoiding responsibility and serious participation in life allows a child or teen to escape feelings of inadequacy. Irresponsibility is often accompanied by substance abuse. When teens or young adults are drugged, others demand less of them, and they are freed from the burdens of being responsible. Irresponsible teens may insist on more freedom, but they make no constructive use of the time or opportunities. They are likely to be tardy, truant, undependable, inefficient, or negligent in performing tasks and responsibilities.

> Underneath irresponsibility and negligence are feelings of incompetence.

Underneath it all, there are feelings of incompetence, a fear of being overwhelmed by life's demands, and a feeling of being unable to meet other people's standards. Being irresponsible on purpose is a way the child can thumb her nose at her parents. As long as she doesn't seriously try, there can be no true failure, no sting of incompetence, no guilt burden about duties still to be performed. If parents complain, the child can always use the magic escape-hatch phrase "I don't care!"—a favorite of oppositional children and teens.

Understand Oppositional Defiant Disorder

DEFIANT BEHAVIOR APPEARS in a wide range of severity. In its most minor form, a child might drag her feet or act lazy—a common and mildly passive-aggressive approach to defying authority. Sporadic laziness and occasional talking back don't warrant clinical intervention.

But the extreme case of a child or teen obsessed with displaying personal power merits a psychiatric diagnosis of oppositional defiant disorder (ODD). Like ADHD and many other psychiatric diagnostic labels, this one is basically a judgment call by the psychologist or other diagnostician. There are no blood, urine, or brain measurement tests that can definitely rule it in or out.

The basic indicators are negativistic, defiant, disobedient, and hostile behaviors toward authority figures that last for at least six months and involve frequent displays of at least four of the following tendencies:

1. Losing temper

2. Arguing with adults

3. Actively defying or refusing to comply with the requests or rules of adults

4. Deliberately doing things that will annoy other people

5. Blaming others for his own mistakes or misbehavior

6. Being touchy or easily annoyed by others

7. Being angry and resentful

8. Being spiteful or vindictive

To qualify for a diagnosis of ODD, these behaviors must occur at abnormally high frequency for children of comparable age and developmental level. They must also lead to significant impairment in social and family relationships, school performance, or job functioning.

There may be consistent stubbornness, resistance to directions, and unwillingness to compromise, give in, or even

Is There Power in Saying No?

Use this clever exercise to understand the great power the oppositional child or teen can experience simply by saying no to whatever the parent requests or orders.

You and a partner—your spouse, or anyone else who is concerned about your child's opposition—face one another.

Your partner will say the word *yes,* using as many different inflections and tones of voice as he can devise. You do the opposite. Each time your partner says *yes,* you are to say *no* with an equally varied assortment of tone and inflection. Do this exercise for 45 seconds.

Then switch.

Allow another 45 seconds of this dialogue and see who wins the "contest" between yes and no. Then discuss the results. Almost invariably, participants experience no as being the more powerful word.

negotiate. There might also be frequent testing of limits, ignoring orders, arguing, and failing to accept blame for misdeeds (externalization).

Hostility can be directed at adults or peers and is considered to be occurring when the child deliberately annoys others or uses verbal aggression to an excessive degree. ODD symptoms almost always occur in the home setting and often start to show up a bit later at school or in the community. Usually, these children and teens don't regard themselves as oppositional or defiant but justify their behavior as a response to unreasonable demands or circumstances placed upon them by adults.

In boys, ODD is more prevalent among those who had symptoms of ADHD in the preschool years. During the school years, there may be low self-esteem, moodiness, low frustration tolerance, swearing, and the use of alcohol, tobacco, or illicit drugs.

Estimates of the incidence of ODD vary from 2 percent of all children and teens having this condition to 16 percent having it. Symptoms usually occur before age 8 but can be noticed for the first time as late as early adulthood. The conflicts created by ODD behavior can involve any authority figure (parent, teacher, supervisor) as well as peers.

Whether or not a strongly oppositional child merits this particular diagnosis, the information in this book will be helpful in improving the adjustment of the child, as well as the family.

Meet ODD's Big Brother: Conduct Disorder

OPPOSITIONAL DEFIANT DISORDER is the stepping stone to juvenile delinquency. While it paves the way for the development of truly delinquent and precriminal activity, ODD generally reflects a condition in which children confine their misbehavior to self-harming and verbal antics.

Typically, ODD misbehavior does not include violent physical aggression toward people, abuse of animals, use of weapons, fire setting, wholesale rejection of societal values, inability to have emotional attachments, destruction of property (vandalism), or a pattern of theft or profound deceit. These traits, and many other characteristics of criminals and delinquents, are included under the psychiatric diagnosis of

Is ODD Inherited?

There is limited research evidence that at least some parts of ODD may be inherited. It is more prevalent in families with:

- Significant marital conflict or divorce
- Child care disrupted by a succession of different caregivers
- Harsh, inconsistent, abusive, or neglectful parenting
- One or both parents having a mood disorder, ODD, conduct disorder, depression, ADHD, antisocial personality disorder, or a substance-related disorder

conduct disorder. This diagnosis encompasses all features of ODD, plus many more serious behavior patterns that indicate severely impaired development of conscience.

Children and teens with extreme cases of oppositional defiant disorder often deteriorate in many aspects of their self-control and emotional health. Here are some of the most common signs of profound ODD. These children and teens will probably develop more serious psychiatric conditions such as conduct disorder if they:

- Destroy property through vandalism or fire setting

- Hurt and harm animals, children, teens, or adults

- Show profound concern with their own comfort

- Withdraw from organized play or group activities

- Run away repeatedly

- Are sloppy or bizarre in appearance

- Shoplift, burglarize, or commit other crimes

- Bully weaker, vulnerable victims

- Physically aggress and have grudge fights

- Don't empathize with others because "it didn't happen to me"

- Frequently use drugs or alcohol

- Show short-term hedonism; emphasize pleasure-of-the-moment

- Have little empathy for hurt or discomfort in others

- Show little fear of withdrawal of care or love by others

- Respond to punishment by becoming more defiant or revengeful

- Desire "freedom" but show no constructive use of time or choices

Oppositional defiant disorder is the stepping stone to juvenile delinquency.

- Show little striving for realistic, positive long-term goals

- Put on "masks"; act two-faced

- Exploit and use others for their own purposes

- Have a "What's in it for me?" attitude

- Show naive optimism and exaggerated faith in their own abilities

- Are reckless about consequences

- Think "What if I pull it off?" rather than "What if I get caught?"

- Like to witness or cause others' suffering

- Trick and con people

- Have an abnormally high risk-taking tendency; devil-may-care propensities

- Destroy, attack, and ridicule things or people

- Seldom self-sacrifice; have little or no inclination for true giving

- Seem unable to show love

- Care little about what others think

- Enjoy shocking and dismaying others

- Are extremely competitive; cruel, arrogant winners; bitter losers

- Are strangely unemotional, composed, and calm in very stressful or violent situations

- Want to appear in control at all times

- Want to prove that nothing bothers or scares them

- Are manipulative in intent when courteous or generous

- Accuse others of acting from sociopathic motives

- Experience sexuality as promiscuous, predatory, or exploitative; no true warmth or emotional closeness

It is important to consult the services of a skilled mental health professional if your child or teen shows any of these traits.

Also seek help for children who merit or whom you suspect might merit any of the diagnoses mentioned in this chapter.

Once you perceive the scope of the many options your child has for displaying illegitimate power, you are in a better position to counteract your child's antics. Watch for the associated features of oppositionality and carefully read the rest of this book for hundreds of practical answers to these types of difficulties. The next chapter gives detailed help for ripping the rug out from under any child's craving for excess power.

3

Create Greater Emotional Safety

T HE FIRST STEP in preventing an unquenchable thirst for power is to keep your child's needs balanced, particularly the four basic needs introduced in chapter 1. This chapter reviews in greater detail how to help meet both the need for belonging and the need for autonomy. When both are met, your child will experience encouragement about self and life. When one or the other is not met, your child will experience discouragement, which will lead to oppositionality.

Oppositionality Reflects Unmet Needs

WITH OPPOSITIONAL CHILDREN and teens, all roads lead back to their needfulness. They can't allow themselves to trust that others in general, and authority figures in particular, will create a safe-enough environment. So they have a profound need to play it safe. They must be assured that they will get all their needs met and not be hurt in the process. Their solution is to make a play for all the power they can get and use it to keep others at an emotional distance while attempting to manipulate things to their advantage.

The best way to rewrite this whole game plan is to approach it from several directions. I describe these approaches in this chapter and each of the remaining chapters of this book.

Upgrade Emotional Safety

THE FIRST STEP is to make the emotional environment healthier. Fulfill needs by launching better processes at home, at school, and in any organized activities in which the child or teen participates. In other words, upgrade the quality of your child's or teen's life, at least insofar as emotional safety is concerned. With emotional safety assured, there is no longer a need for an elaborate scheme to usurp power and manipulate people through oppositionality.

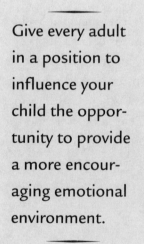

Give every adult in a position to influence your child the opportunity to provide a more encouraging emotional environment.

Your child is valuable. This project requires and deserves a team effort. Give every adult in a relevant position to influence your child the opportunity to provide a more encouraging emotional environment. The teacher should read this chapter, as should the counselor or psychologist, the child care provider, the scout or church youth group leader, and any other adults in a position to have ongoing interaction with your child or teen.

The Twin Functions of Effective Parenting

SUPPOSE YOU ARE going to buy a wiener roast fork. You want one with two tines of similar length—about 5 inches. Imagine each tine as one of the two essential aspects of high-quality, encouraging adult leadership. The tine on the left represents love; the tine on the right represents guidance.

Now imagine a wiener roast fork with a 20-inch tine and a 1-inch tine. Too much love (the 20-inch tine) combined with insufficient guidance (the 1-inch tine) can be stifling and damaging. This is the family where a child is raised with overprotection, overindulgence, nagging, and pitying—the combination of which is destructive to the child's emotional growth. The spoiled, pampered child who is given into becomes a power-drunk tyrant toward his beleaguered, guilt-ridden parents.

Reversing the tines can be equally destructive. In this situation, you have a fork with too much guidance (the 20-inch tine) combined with insufficient love (the 1-inch tine). The result is harsh, punitive discipline and emotional rejection of the child. Relying heavily on punishment and criticism whenever the child misbehaves sabotages emotional growth and the development of conscience.

Now imagine a wiener roast fork with two short tines about 1 inch long. An insufficient amount of love, combined with insufficient guidance, is a seedbed for raising a juvenile delinquent who has almost no sense of moral obligation toward others.

And, of course, there's the fork with two 30-inch tines—one where the parent or other adult completely smothers a child with attention, intervention, interaction, and unwanted guidance. This unstable combination results in children who, quite appropriately, throw off smothering adults and build walls that give them some breathing space. Children who are smothered by overinvolved adults are often perceived as defiant when they are, in fact, simply trying to become autonomous.

The only combination of the two functions that works well is to have an appropriate amount of both love and guidance—two 5-inch tines. Emotionally healthy parents convey love in meaningful ways that impart a deep sense of being cherished and being appreciated. They encourage healthy amounts of independence and personal growth. At the same time, they provide credible guidance that gives direction without undercutting the child's sense of being loved.

Other Tools

NOW THAT I'VE clarified how to balance the two most significant aspects of raising children and teenagers, it's time to implement some specific relationship tools for developing functional, loving children who care about the people in their lives. As you introduce these tools into your family or classroom, continue to be mindful of the balance and length of the two "tines" of love and guidance.

Have your tool belt strapped on? The following are the tools you'll need to build a strong, functional family unit.

Take the lead. This is your family, your classroom, your group. As the adult leader, you are responsible for how it functions. If you are the parent in a family with an oppositional child, hold regular family meetings—just as you would if you led any other organization. Moreover, parents should hold leadership meetings, in private, to discuss the way the family is to be led. In private conversation, parents can resolve their parenting differences so that they can take a united approach to raising children.

Meet regularly, too, with your children as a group. In weekly or biweekly family council meetings, make the necessary decisions for keeping order and smooth functioning of the processes necessary for running a family or any other group with defiant children. Somebody has to be minding the store, even if you have a disruptive oppositional child in the midst.

A caution: Do *not* allow family meetings to degenerate into unkind, critical, "Why don't you ever . . . ?" sessions. These meetings need to be optimistic, full of admiration for one another's best attributes, and focused on the future rather than the past. Work together to find appropriate guidelines for the family; do not rehash old mistakes, which should have been dealt with privately and completely resolved prior to the family meeting.

Share some of the burden. Don't put all the blame on the child for making everything problematic and don't demand that the child do all the "shaping up." Be willing to hunt for changes and improvements you can do to improve your half of all the two-person relationships you are involved with in your family.

> Family meetings need to be optimistic, full of admiration for one another's best attributes, and focused on the future rather than the past.

Don't rely on pure authority. If your child gave you instant compliant cooperation, you would have no need for this book. But why bother with a whole book full of ideas about how to get along with an oppositional, defiant child? At first glance, it would seem a simple matter to order the child to cooperate based on your authority as the parent or adult leader. Unfortunately, things don't work that way. It would be nice if they did.

Trying to overwhelm a resistant, defiant child with your authority will result in little other than pure backlash rebellion. You can, however, add other tools to supplement your legitimate authority so that it becomes a contributing ingredient to the total influence you have on your child. Your authority should be part of the picture, but don't try to make it the whole picture.

Give Your Child License to Express Feelings

THERE IS AN important leadership tool that requires more in-depth consideration. If you have a defiant child, it's very likely that both you and the child have difficulties with appropriate expression of emotions. In this section, I explain how to restore healthy emotional expression.

Children enjoy the excitement and wonder of the world and of life. Those who have a safe, supportive, and helpful family setting usually grow up with a healthy kind of emotional expressiveness. Sometimes, though, a child discovers that this naturally clear way of expressing personal needs becomes dangerous or profitless. Under attack from painful and scary interactions with others, the child learns to handle feelings in the opposite way—to hide, distort, under- or overstate, and not reveal or even not be aware of whatever should be felt and experienced.

Promote the freedom to feel. People who are able to express their emotions are genuine. They don't resort to lies or tricks when dealing with others. Parents who provide a supportive emotional setting for their children's natural honesty of emotional expression can do much to strengthen and enrich their children's life experiences.

Here is how to help any child maintain or regain that point-blank emotional honesty. Ideally this "freedom to feel," combined with the child's natural friendliness, helps the child get along with others. It is important to give your child a license to express genuine feelings—to be "real" with you. This skill will be useful in all other relationships your child will ever experience.

Follow your feelings. The child is usually expressing genuine emotional needs through oppositionality. If you handle your own emotions in a healthy manner, you set up a model for your children to develop the freedom to have, recognize, express, and benefit from feelings. Believe it or not, feelings are at the crux of most family-related problems having to do with defiance and oppositional misbehavior.

Feelings are generally a good, reliable guide to adjustment. We should follow our feelings; they point us on the road to happiness and fulfillment. Even an oppositional child should be following those feelings, but in a more socially appropriate way than the patterns of power seeking described in the preceding chapter.

Tune in to your child's feelings. The renowned family therapist Virginia Satir taught that the great myth of childhood is "If my parents don't know what I need, they don't love me!" It is important that your child not succumb to this myth. Don't let your child conclude that you don't love or care about him simply because he hasn't conveyed his genuine feelings to you clearly. Make sure that you understand your child's wants. This chapter and chapter 4 provide extensive coverage of how to "read" your child's emotions more clearly.

Encourage journaling. If your child seems to have trouble conveying feelings, a diary or journal can sometimes help clarify what is enjoyable and what is troublesome about life. While a

The Joys of Journaling

When dealing with an oppositional child, it's tough to find moments of joy. Lisa is the mother of a highly opposi- tional son who is now 18 years old. While much of their relationship is turbulent—the combination of defiance and teenage hormones are lethal—Lisa and her son, Thomas, have a few warm spots that give strength to their otherwise fragile bond. One of the things that keeps Lisa going is a journal she began keeping when Thomas first began talking. Every once in a while, Lisa pulls out that old journal, and Thomas sits down beside her on the couch for a good laugh. A favorite entry—dictated by Thomas when he was four years old—says "When I grow up I'm going to get married, and the name of my wife will be Mary Sue Tigershark." Lisa says the smartest thing she ever did was to put together baby books and journals for Thomas because they're tangible proof that no matter how frustrating life gets, Thomas is loved, and there's a good kid underneath all that defiance and teen angst.

diary should remain private, the child can refer to it when you discuss how things are going. A journal is a diary that is shared with parents or a counselor. If your child doesn't know where to begin, have her start by writing down moments of especially pleasant or "good" feelings as well as the moments of especially unpleasant ones—the highs and the lows of each day.

Give license to be real. Surprise! Surprise! Your teen may at times act just like a teen! It may sound like common sense, but

well-meaning parents sometimes overlook this principle. Don't expect more than your child can give. Expect childishness and immaturity—not a level of functioning you'd expect from a miniature adult. After all, if children could spring full-blown into adulthood, they wouldn't require parents!

At the same time, though, all teens want more say in how their life is being run and have a natural need for increasing independence. In fact, their most important need is to define themselves as separate, unique entities from their parents.

Provide Powerful Encouragement for Your Child

IMAGINE A FOUR-LEGGED table, with each leg representing an important element of encouragement for any child or teen. If a leg is cut or broken, the table can't support the weight or burdens of life. The child is likely to malfunction and misbehave. It is important to see to it that you send messages supporting your child's strong sense of belonging, represented by two of the legs, as well as a strong sense of autonomy, represented by the other two legs. The following are the four key messages to send to your child.

Leg #1: Belonging—Social Impact

THE CHILD WHO has a strong sense of this belonging message feels noticed and appreciated and senses that his contributions matter to others. Your child will gain a greater sense of connecting and "fitting in" by virtue of being more aware of how his efforts are impacting others.

> All teens want more say in how their life is being run and have a natural need for increasing independence.

Promote conscience development. Anything you can do to help conscience grow stronger will lessen the likelihood of oppositionality in your child. Conscience consists of awareness of and concern about one's impact on other people and their feelings. Showing your child exactly how his actions favorably impact on others builds conscience. A strong conscience mitigates against the development of oppositional tendencies.

Pay attention. You want your child to develop a belief that his parents and other adults and children pay attention to him, express interest in his needs and wants, and listen to him. The best way to build up that expectation is to make it happen in real life. Do you convey your interest in the things your child does and is interested in?

Show appreciation. Appreciate and thank him for his contributions and helpful actions. Give specific feedback about how the action benefited you or someone else: "By doing that favor for me, you made it possible for me to make that important phone call. Thank you." Take time to give "thank you" messages expressing your own gratitude as well as gratitude on behalf of others, particularly on behalf of those who can't express themselves.

Don't forget animal impact. Always consider animals to be symbolic of humans. Social impact extends to animals. If children care for a pet, they have a positive impact on the animal. Point it out and thank them for it.

Urge sharing and cooperation. It is important to give your child a strong sense of belonging by reinforcing his awareness of the direct favorable impact he has on others. For example, if your child picks up trash from a pathway and deposits it in a trash can, he deserves acknowledgment. He needs to know that his contribution makes a positive difference in how smoothly society functions. Encourage cooperative, sharing behavior. Teach him that his cooperation is needed to help fulfill particular needs. Urge sharing so that he learns the value of contributing for the benefit of all.

Promote peer group activities. Ask your child's teachers to invite him to participate on committees and team assignments at school and in other group situations. Encourage your child to take part in extracurricular clubs, church groups, and community organizations. Working together with others toward a common goal provides fertile ground for the seeds of both belonging and social impact. Being accepted into peer groups teaches your child that others have need of his cooperation.

Leg #2: Belonging—Self-Worth

THE CHILD WHO has a strong sense of this belonging message feels cherished and deeply loved and senses that his very presence matters to others. To help provide this form of encouragement, demonstrate your love for your child.

Show unconditional cherishing. The love children feel should be unconditional, not dependent on whether they were "good" recently. Give gifts, do favors, and express your love at times other than when expected and without consideration for your child's pattern of behavior. Arrange to spend special time together. Find frequent opportunities to do something together for fun. Children and teenagers are encouraged if they perceive that parents and the other significant adults in their lives want to be with them, talk to them, and enjoy their company.

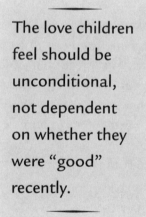

The love children feel should be unconditional, not dependent on whether they were "good" recently.

Treat your child as valuable. Demonstrate that your child has infinite worth and is very precious. Provide assistance when the going gets rough. Consider at least a partial rescue from situations in which your child might become hurt or threatened in some way. For example, if your child is bullied or harassed, intervene on his behalf. Assist him in times of difficulty and protect him from danger, injury, or harm. In general, show him the courtesy and respect you would show any valued, cherished, deeply loved person in your life.

Show empathy for feelings. Use sophisticated, high-level communication processes such as active listening and empathy, which indicate deep and abiding respect for your child.

The best way to handle feelings expressed by your child is with the kid gloves of empathy.

Empathy is emotional salve. It is the safest response to give to anyone who is expressing a sincere feeling. Giving empathy validates your child's feelings and conveys your interest and your caring. It forms the basis for a bridge of understanding that undercuts the child's tendency to be oppositional. Chapter 4 provides detailed guidance in developing emotional communication that deters oppositionality.

Show respect and courtesy. The best way to obtain your child's respect is to model it. Take actions that uphold the child's basic dignity and self-respect. Getting children and teens to communicate requires that they have respect for their parents. Such respect is seldom gained through demands, orders, threats, and punishments. It is more easily gained by earning it through first showing basic kindness, decency, and courtesy.

Common errors made by parents include yelling at a child in front of his friends, borrowing from the child without repaying or returning the item or the money, and breaking promises. If you expect the child to ask before borrowing something of yours, return the favor when you borrow. Respect privacy by not opening mail, eavesdropping on phone conversations, or peeking at the child's e-mail.

Leg #3: Autonomy—Self-Direction

THE CHILD WHO has a strong sense of this autonomy message feels powerful and influential and senses that his wants matter to others. He has faith that his parents and other adults give him a voice and a choice whenever possible. He feels as if his hands are on the steering wheel of his life and that he can influence the factors that, in turn, affect him. He doesn't feel dominated or excessively bossed around. He has no difficulty conforming to wants expressed by authority figures. He expects such requests to be fair and to honor his rights to influence his own destiny and express his wants and preferences. He feels free to own and express his wants and feelings in a socially appropriate manner.

This is one of the most important forms of encouragement to provide for the strong-willed, oppositional child or teen. When he experiences a sufficient amount of healthy self-direction, there is little need to go out of his way to claim additional power. Experiencing self-direction means being in charge of one's own life.

There are several aspects to self-direction. Here are areas to emphasize in order to provide this all-important type of encouragement for your child.

Offer a family heritage. An important part of a sense of identity is reflected in an awareness of family heritage. Feeling "part of" an extended family also can have the effect of making teenagers behave responsibly. When the thought of embarrassing Mom or Dad doesn't influence behavior, the idea of disappointing Grandpa, Aunt Ellen, and cousin Tony might do so. In addition, simply believing that a departed relative cares about and watches over a child can help that child feel loved and draw him back into the family. The impact of extended family can't be overstated. Adults who grew up as adoptees, for example, often have a gnawing urge to reclaim their origins by making the acquaintance of their birth parents. Often, of course, such reunions are tragic. But their frequent occurrence testifies to the universality of the need to be aware of, and in some sense claim ownership of, one's heritage. Perhaps there are ways in which you can strengthen your child's sense of enjoyment and participation in familywide activities such as genealogical awareness, reunions, looking through memoirs from ancestors, and similar activities. Don't forget holidays as opportunities to show family movies and slides and to assemble picture albums and family scrapbooks.

Emphasize uniqueness. Anything you can do to highlight your child's unique preferences, tastes, talents, and ways of doing things will reinforce his sense of personal autonomy. Part of uniqueness is self-acceptance. Your child has certain traits that are predetermined and not the result of free choice, such as racial and ethnic affiliation, hair and eye color, body build, and similar features of the self. Ideally, your child should accept these traits as ingredients going into the total entity called "me." There should be no embarrassment or self-disdain about these aspects of self.

Permission to establish his preferred decor in his room helps any child feel a greater sense of autonomy. Room decor is a convenient area in which to provide significant opportunities for self-expression.

Another important gesture loving parents make is creating a "baby book" for their children. It's never too late to create a record of an individual child's life. Even teenagers—who might pretend to roll their eyes and scorn the effort—can't help but feel cherished when a parent cares enough about that child to remember his birth, mark his development, and memorialize his accomplishments.

Respect physical requirements and capabilities. It is important to teach your child how to show respect for his own needs. If he functions better on 10 hours of sleep, provide for that amount of sleep. If he does better with a protein-rich breakfast—something that is true for most children with ADHD—arrange for it.

Help your child become aware of the limits of his capabilities so that he has a clear sense of when to accomplish tasks without help and when to ask for assistance. Ideally, your child should be able to write down a list of 10 things he is really good at and 10 things he is not good at but wishes he were better at doing. And he should be able to have a smile on his face while writing both lists. In other words, your child should be at peace with the unique configuration of talents and limitations with which he is endowed. Help him revel in his strengths and compensate calmly for his weaknesses. Neither should be exaggerated or overemphasized by you or by your child.

Honor rights and feelings. If your child wants privacy, give it. Knock before entering his room. Address him with politeness. Set an example of being in tune with your child's feelings and basic right to be treated with kindness and dignity. The way is then open for you to expect the same from your child in regard to how he treats others. By showing respect for your child's rights and feelings as part of his uniqueness, you earn it in return, and oppositionality decreases.

Reinforce choice-making power. If you want your child to be less argumentative and contrary, make sure he has ample opportunity to exercise free will and self-determination. Decide on several areas in which you can afford to allow your child more personal discretion and influence. Common areas include choosing from among several household chores, bedtime and arising time, food preferences, room decor, hairstyle, and clothing choices. You should not, of course, abandon your leadership role, and you have the right and responsibility to set limits on your child. But open up any available opportunities for legitimate choice making. If you don't deal your child some power cards, your child will grab power by becoming oppositional.

What Bugs Your Child About You?

The teacher in a family living class at a suburban Chicago elementary school surveyed the most common complaints from over 5,000 children and came up with a list of the 25 most "unwanted" things parents do to kids. Of those, seven are very relevant to this aspect of encouragement. Children are very bothered when their parents:

- Make you break your plans to do something the parent wants to do
- Don't consult you about movies, shopping lists, preferred food
- Throw out your old toys and clothes without consulting you
- Force you to eat food you don't like
- Invite your friends over without consulting you
- Don't ask your advice or take your suggestions
- Sign you up for lessons or classes without consulting you

All seven involve denying children legitimate choice and influence and are likely to propel a child into oppositionality.

Reinforce responsibility. Show your child that he can influence his own destiny by the choices he makes. Don't let him dodge the bullet of responsibility by externalizing either the blame or the credit for whatever he does. His actions are always the result of his choices. Make sure he understands that fact. If he eats vegetables, he will stay healthy; if he dabbles in drugs, he will get in trouble. If he doesn't study, he will fail tests. If he is kind to his dog, the dog will return the kindness. The autonomous person knows and accepts the basic immutable law of life that natural consequences will automatically kick in in response to every choice he makes. This is a central focus for experiencing personal power, so emphasize it for your child.

Allow self-determined pacing. Your child should determine his speed and amount of effort in doing things based on his own perceptions, needs, and body states. How others do things should mostly be irrelevant. Give reassurances such as:

- Work at a pace that is comfortable for you

- Don't go any faster or slower than you want to

- Never mind how others are doing; just go at your own pace

> Your child's talents are best developed based on the timetable of her own personal enjoyment, not on pressure from a parent.

In contrast, externally determined pacing is discouraging and leads to oppositionality. With external pacing, the child's pace of work is determined by the parents or teacher. It might also be determined by how others are doing, through comparison and competition. Competition is discouraging to both the winner and the loser.

Be careful with lessons. Getting an oppositional child involved in activities that allow the experience of increasing personal strength, competence, and choice-making power is a good idea. Encourage but don't force participation in music, dance, crafts, athletics, or martial arts pro-

Do You Gear Expectations to Readiness?

Always adjust what you ask of your child to whatever your child appears "ready" for. Imagine three parent-child pairs in a park. The first parent yanks the child along, scolding the child for walking too slowly. The second parent walks too slowly for the child so that the child tugs and pulls the sluggish parent along. These two parents are not in concert with their children's readiness.

The third pair, however, is very different from the other two in that there is no conflict. The parent and child are walking along at a pace comfortable for both. When either wants to move faster or slower, a brief mention is made, and that need is recognized and discussed by both. Together, they make a mutually agreed upon adjustment in their pace.

The third pair represents how you should be pacing the responsibilities and challenges for your child. Listen to your child's honest feelings about what is happening day-to-day. Gear your expectations in a way that is fine-tuned to your child.

grams. Talents are best developed based on the timetable of the child's own personal enjoyment, not on pressure from a parent.

Leg #4: Autonomy—Self-Confidence

THE CHILD WHO has a strong sense of this autonomy message is self-accepting and satisfied with his strengths and talents and senses that his efforts truly matter. He can list his strengths without arrogance, egotism, perfectionism, or grandiosity. And he can list the chief areas of weakness or shortcoming that he wishes he were better at without self-hate, embarrassment, or depression.

He has a strong self-acceptance of his unique configuration of skills and abilities. He senses that he can pass muster in life and meet the obligations and tasks placed before him by authority figures—his parents, teachers, and employers.

Emphasize enjoyment. It is a common but misguided notion that you should praise children in order to have them feel good about their accomplishments. I recommend that you de-emphasize the quality of their performance rather than draw attention to it. Your child will become much more encouraged, for example, if you focus on his enjoyment of whatever he is doing. Say, for instance, "The important thing is that you enjoy yourself. Don't worry about your score."

The discouraging opposite is to give no mention of the child's enjoyment level and focus on quality of performance. "You did a good job" conveys judgment, not love.

Compare with past performance. The child should compare his past performance with his current performance to gauge the speed or quality of his efforts. Note that this type of feedback contrasts with competition, in which his performance is gauged against that of other people. To help provide this form of encouragement, use "super strokes" on the opposite page rather than judgmental praise.

Avoid perfectionism. The best thing to do with a mistake is learn from it. Teach your child to have a realistic, uplifted attitude about personal accomplishments. When commenting on successes, avoid the two damaging Ps: perfectionism and judgmental praise. Children and teens need an emotional climate where mistakes are tolerated. A child can't be taught to take care of himself unless you let him try to take care of himself. Your

Super Strokes

by John F. Taylor, Ph.D.

Super strokes are statements and actions that tend to develop, maintain, or enhance the child's experiencing of self-worth, social impact, self-direction, or self-confidence.

1. GRATITUDE: "Thank you!" "I am grateful for what you did."

2. SHARING A SKILL: "Now you can play pretty music for all of us." "Are there any other students whom you can help in math now?"

3. EMPATHY: "I'll bet that was fun." "You really enjoy doing that, don't you?"

4. SOCIAL IMPACT: "When you did that, it allowed me to rest 5 minutes." "You really helped Suzy by doing that."

5. RECIPROCAL FAVOR: "I'm sure Matt will want to play with you tomorrow since you played so nicely today." "When you help with the dishes, I have more time for playing with you."

6. UNIQUENESS: "Green is really your color." "Your suns always have such happy smiles."

7. SELF-DETERMINATION: "I would like you to do this, but you choose how and when." "You go right ahead if that is what you want."

8. SELF-IMPACT: "There are lots of things you can do to help yourself." "You're helping yourself by doing that." "Jogging will strengthen your heart and lungs." "It's nice to do something for yourself, isn't it?"

9. MATERIAL IMPACT: "You can build a lot of things with your new tool kit." "When you water the flowers, they will grow and bloom."

10. ACKNOWLEDGE EFFORT: "I can see a lot of work went into this." "I'm glad you tried."

11. LABEL THE ACT: "You tied your shoes." "You cleaned your room." "You drew me a picture."

12. EMPHASIZE STRENGTH: "This is easier for you now." "Your correct answers are circled in red." "That part looked easy for you."

13. TELL ME ABOUT IT: "Tell me about your picture." "I'm interested to hear what you are doing in school."

Developed by John F. Taylor, Ph.D. Permission granted to reproduce this form. Call 1-800-847-1233 for a free catalog.

A New Definition of Success

You can head west from any point on earth, but there is no specific location that is completely "west." The same is true of perfection. You can always head toward it by trying harder and practicing more. But you can never arrive at being perfect; nobody is ever perfect in anything.

I have a new definition of success for your child: any heading west. An event is a success if, for example, your child learns from it for the next time.

---

child will make mistakes, and out of these can come wisdom and self-discipline.

Strengthen the bond with your child. One way to undercut oppositional tendencies in children is to keep your bond of affection strong. In times of potential conflict, you can refer to your loving bond. Remind your child that you have enjoyed a close, affectionate relationship and ask him not to spoil it by insisting on his way regardless of the needs of others.

Give love by surprise. Find clever ways to express your love by means other than hugs and kisses. Notes describing pleasant surprises can be included in each child's lunch or jacket pocket. The surprises can include favors and privileges, such as a restaurant meal or a movie rental.

Thoughtful deeds that come as an unannounced surprise can often be memorable and precious highlights for a child or teen. A good-tasting snack from the kitchen, delivered as a surprise gift, is almost unbeatable as a way to help a child feel loved. The answer to "What are these cookies for?" is "Because I love you."

Pair off together. Each parent should spend some time alone with each child, allowing her to bask in the undiluted love and attention of the parent. Do a high-energy activity together that is recreational in nature and suited to your child's interests.

This method is ideal for children who are not ready or able to accept more direct and intimate forms of affection from their parents. It is also well suited for parents who are not very demonstrative in giving physical displays of affection.

I recommend the simple formula "Each parent, each child, each week." At least once per week, each child gets a special time together with each parent. For busy families, a restaurant breakfast or a morning jog together would be good examples.

Give a great tuck-in. Children and teens are amazingly receptive to adult input as part of bedtime tuck-in. I always advise parents to take advantage of tuck-ins. Bedtime is an ideal time to express your love and interest. Do a day's review, ask your child to share the highs and lows of the day with you, and remind your child of your love. You can use this opportunity to discuss further any events during the day in which your child displayed inappropriate power-seeking misbehavior. Your discussion should be brief, calm, and consist mostly of explaining how your child's antics are lose-lose events that don't benefit anybody. I discuss this approach in detail in chapter 6.

> I always advise parents to take advantage of tuck-ins. Bedtime is an ideal time to express your love and interest.

Tuck-in should never be longer than 15 minutes and should not exhaust you. It should include some loving touch such as a back rub. If you are near end-of-rope level in energy or mood, however, don't attempt a

The Absolute Grand-Prize Winner

If I were giving the All-Time-Greatest-Way Grand Prize for preventing or reducing oppositionality, I would give it to a simple interview procedure. I call it the personal private interview, or PPI.

Pretend you are a news reporter and interview your child about everything in his life. Find out how he is doing, what is going well and what isn't, how he feels about the chores and allowance arrangements, any current needs for the supplies of daily living such as school supplies or clothes, and issues and concerns your child has.

The "issues and concerns" part is the most important for preventing oppositionality. Have your child maintain a small notebook, for use during your PPI, in which he writes down all issues. If you help find a win-win solution to every issue, you will prevent many problems from ever developing.

tuck-in. Have audiotapes available with relaxation narration, music, or bedtime stories for those nights when a personal tuck-in is inadvisable or impractical.

Strengthen Togetherness in Your Family

HERE ARE SOME ways to upgrade everyone's sense of connection in your family. To the extent that a child feels emotionally bonded to siblings, conscience is strengthened and selfishness lessens. The more of these activities you can develop, the less oppositional your child is likely to become.

Express gratitude. Find occasions to thank your children for doing things. Doing small favors provides ways for everyone in the family to show their love for each other on a daily basis. Giving "thank you" messages is one of the "super strokes" and therefore is a powerful encouragement to provide for any child.

Have weekly fun time. Take the phone off the hook, unplug the TV, serve some fun food, and play some family games together. Protect the fun times against outside interruptions and urge attendance by everyone. Invest this half-hour once a week and watch the payoffs as they transpire throughout the week.

Use holidays wisely. Make every holiday a chance for the entire family to discover more ways to enjoy each other. Take advantage of the special meals and get-togethers to upgrade your child's sense of connection with family members. Involve your children in making greeting cards for each other. Help your children buy or create thoughtful gifts for one another. Holidays are a terrific opportunity to teach compassion and sensitivity within your family.

Celebrate your family. Have pictures of family members on the walls of your home. Put trophies, school certificates, and other memorabilia on display. Be alert for opportunities to give all family members a greater sense of family pride.

Conduct cooperative ventures. Work and play together with the common goal of cooperation and companionship. Projects should involve something the entire family—or at least many family members—can pitch in on together.

Have special days. Give each family member a day to be "king" or "queen" and to do just about anything, including being free of the usual responsibilities and obligations. The child can have a special table setting, wear a special hat, have favorite meals, and choose family fun activities for that evening.

Encourage cooperative play. Competition always feeds into oppositionality, and cooperation defuses it. A regular playtime has several advantages for you and your children and can be of great help in strengthening your family and reducing oppositionality.

Cooperative games differ from competitive games in that the factor of persons being pitted against each other is minimized or absent. Instead of a winner who defeats a loser, all players work toward a common goal. All players win if the goal is reached, and all lose if the goal is not reached.

The goal might be that all players finish their parts of the game at the same time. In cooperative Chinese checkers, for example, all players try to place their last marbles into home place on the same round. If your children insist on competitive card and table games, try to minimize the level of competition by having the less-skilled player receive a head start or a lower goal in order to win. You want the outcome to be distributed at just about a chance level among the players.

Understand your own emotions. As much as possible in talking with your child, express your feelings in a direct, honest, and flowing manner. Combining your emotions with straight thinking and reasonable judgment is the best approach to model for your child.

Name, Claim, Tame, and Aim

THE CORRECT HEALTHY handling of emotions involves four steps. Teach these steps to your children and model their use by your own example:

Name it. Identify the emotions you are feeling. Often you will be experiencing two or three simultaneous feelings. It may

CREATE GREATER EMOTIONAL SAFETY • 85

help to imagine what a picture that symbolized how you are feeling would be like.

Claim it. Don't blame your child or anyone else for the way you feel. Own your feelings. The simple statement, "I feel . . . when you . . ." is a good starting point.

Tame it. Combine self-control and alert thinking with what you are feeling. Think to yourself "What would be the best win-win action to take to solve this problem?" Put your brain in gear over the matter because acting out of pure emotion seldom solves things.

> Competition always feeds into oppositionality, and cooperation defuses it.

Aim it. The best way to handle "negative" feelings is to transform them into "positive" actions and assert your needs in a calm way. Negatively experienced emotions are warning signals alerting you to change something. Direct your energy in a way that will help relieve the emotional pain you are experiencing. Always hunt for a win-win way to resolve unpleasant feelings, never a win-lose way.

Honest naming, claiming, taming, and aiming of your feelings aids family harmony, promotes clear emotional communication, and sets a wonderful example. Speaking of examples . . .

Set an Example

PROBABLY THE MOST potent influence on how oppositional children and teenagers handle their own emotions is how parents handle theirs. In trying to help children learn how to deal with their own emotions, you will be using the teaching tool of your own example more than any other method.

I've noted that children mirror their parents' response to stress. If the parent expresses frustration and resentment about a certain situation, the child will feel angry about it also. In my years of clinical practice, I've known many children who have short fuses and who have even thrown things. Almost invariably, it's turned out that these children have parents who have short fuses and who throw things. Children who take setbacks in stride and learn to find humor in their mistakes often have parents who do the same.

It can be very meaningful and helpful if you will set an example of honesty in displaying emotions. Such an example is one of the most powerful methods of teaching your child or teen how to express his own feelings.

Additional Tools

YOUR NEW PARENTING tool belt isn't quite complete. There are several additional methods of opening communication channels between parents and oppositional children. Parents and other adults who interact with oppositional children and teens will find these tools useful in building their relationship.

Earn your child's trust. Trust is a two-way street. If you want to be trusted, be trustable. Maintain confidentiality when you hear embarrassing or private information from or about your child. Following through with what you say you are going to do, never lying to your child, announcing your genuine feelings and opinions, and openly explaining why you do what you do all help show your trustworthiness. The more trustable you are, the more approachable you will be, from your child's point of view. By paving the way for emotional intimacy, your "trust account" helps ensure against an oppositional reaction from your child.

Treat feelings as valuable. Emotions are basically guiding and protective. They alert us whenever our needs are under threat, and they help us use our defenses and skills to confront or flee from harmful or threatening situations. They also point us in the needed direction to change things for the better.

The fuel gauge on your automobile is not "bad" because it points to "empty." In fact, it is quite helpful. In the same way, your child's emotions are not "bad" because they indicate a state of imbalance or potential threat to having needs met. Treat your child's emotions as very important, special, and pure aspects of his or her being. Remember, a child without emotions would be a robot.

Deal with negatives honestly. Even when your feelings are unpleasant or negative, it is better to display them honestly, openly, directly, and congruently than to hide them, deny them, or try to cover them up. Your child needs to learn to deal with you, which includes the feelings you have. Your child needs a real human being as a model and guide. By being congruent and honest in expressing your emotions, you can give the gift of your own realness to your child.

> Treat your child's emotions as very important, special, and pure aspects of his or her being.

Never openly letting your children know how you actually are affected by their behavior deprives them of some of the tools that they need in order to learn how to handle their relationships with others. Honest announcing of genuine feelings aids family harmony and sets a more useful example than hiding of those feelings.

Meet your own emotional needs. Sometimes, parents have unfulfilled emotional needs that are very demanding. Unable to meet these leftover childhood needs on their own, parents try to force their children to do so. Often, the parents make the child perform functions that should be performed by another person in the parent's life, either past or present. Most of these patterns are offshoots of the dejuvenilization pattern of malparenting discussed in chapter 1. The result is always tragic.

Here are several examples I've seen in my clinical psychology family practice that cause serious emotional overburdening for almost any child. Oppositionality is a natural response for any child experiencing a parent who:

- Uses the child excessively for household responsibilities and as a built-in sitter and caregiver for younger children

- Insists that the child continue lessons or afterschool activities in order to impress relatives

- Uses a daughter or son for comfort and as a "crying towel" while going through a crisis

- Because of feeling very lonely, forces excessive companionship onto a son or daughter

- Babies and spoils the child to maintain the child's dependence

- Behaves and dresses in an inappropriately youthful manner; takes pride in being mistaken for the child's sibling or peer

In these and similar instances of emotional overburdening, the parent is responding more to personal needs than to the needs of the child.

There is nothing wrong with encouraging music or dance lessons or with inviting an older child to clean the kitchen or watch younger siblings briefly—so long as these activities arise out of a genuine and healthy concern for the child's own best interests, rather than the parent's. But when parents act out of primary consideration for their own unmet emotional needs and make the children a secondary priority, they do severe harm to the child's emotional development. Children are not emotionally capable of being small adults or of filling the gap for parents who aren't fully adult. In trying to meet their parents' out-of-balance emotional needs, children have no choice but to leave their own emotional needs unmet, creating large gaps in their emotional growth. The children are forced, in one way or another, to become miniature adults. Their natural self-protective reaction is to become oppositional.

Asking them to fulfill leftover parental needs makes children feel inadequate and guilty for not being able to accomplish what is actually an impossible task. Feeling like a victim adds fuel to the fire of an oppositional nature.

Take steps to correct or lessen any out-of-balance pressure you might be experiencing in your daily life. Never use your child as a substitute for an adult or for working on your own personal growth. If this kind of pressure is occurring, seek skilled professional counseling or psychotherapy.

Expand your parenting knowledge. Participate in parent education courses, group meetings, and programs within your community. Be careful, however, about the content you are offered. Many such courses will send you right into power struggles with an oppositional child or teen. Seek out presenters and leaders whose approach corresponds with the loving guidance approach advocated in this book. One of the best ways to find out whether you're getting the kind of information you really need is to show chapter 6 to the leader and seek a response. The leader will either congratulate you for finding this book or scoff at what chapter 6 says. Then you'll have your answer.

Character flaws can sabotage you. Children won't follow a leader they don't believe. The more credible the adult is, the less oppositional the child. An important part of establishing yourself as a credible parent is being a credible person. Dishonesty, lying, committing any of the abusive malparenting patterns discussed in chapter 1, or showing other evidence of untrustworthiness will hurt. Drug or alcohol abuse and even heavy smoking by a parent also place a heavy burden on any child's ability to love and trust. If addictive substances or any of the malparenting patterns are part of the picture, admit it and get help. Your child doesn't need you to be perfect. Just honest.

Replenish yourself. Dealing with an oppositional child or teen drains energy. You must replenish it. To prevent end-of-rope states and deteriorated levels of parenting, take time out for breaks, rest, a hobby, prayer, meditation, jogging, or whatever other ways work for you. It is vitally important to have regular time away from an especially demanding or problematic child or teen. At least once a week and preferably more often, arrange to refresh and renew yourself away from the home. The timeless remedies of enough sleep and adequate nutrition are also important.

4

Sharpen Your Communication Skills

OPPOSITIONAL AND POWER-PLAY misbehavior occurs more often in families where the parents seldom
communicate with their children and end up nagging
or scolding when they do communicate.

Parents who communicate frequently with their children
about emotionally meaningful topics generally have fewer problems with power struggles and power-oriented misbehavior.

According to research, the most frequent response by teens
to the question of what problems they have in getting along
with their parents is "not being listened to."

Want to get back on track with your child or teen? An excellent starting place is to increase the number of empathic, intimate conversations you have together.

Convey Acceptance

YOUR CHILD HAS a bad day and shouts "I *hate* you!" How do you respond? Your first instinct might be to argue with the child ("No, you don't!") or to retaliate ("Well, I'm not very fond of you either"). Both reactions only escalate the problem and set up a power play.

There's a better way. Rather than defend or retaliate, simply accept and empathize with your child's feelings. You can deal with the consequences *after* you understand the emotion. Regardless of whether you approve of your child's having a particular feeling, show your desire to help her experience, identify or label, then benefit from the feeling.

> Rather than defend or retaliate, simply accept and empathize with your child's feelings.

Acceptance of your child's feeling doesn't mean liking the feeling. Nor does it mean tolerating hostility or abusiveness. It does mean treating the feeling as real and genuine from your child's point of view. Suppose your child expresses anger about a sibling. An accepting response that shows empathy would be: "This is a hard time for you, isn't it? I think I understand how you feel. Are you angry because Sally got to go to Todd's party and you weren't invited?" Notice the question format. Your attentiveness to your child's feelings is best shown by asking whether you are correct in your understanding, rather than assuming that you are.

Another harmful possibility is that your child will start to feel inadequate and unable to do enough to satisfy you. A feeling of rejection occurs if the child thinks that the parent is unaccepting and disapproving. The next step in this unfortunate chain of emotional events is a decrease in the child's affection

What's the Safest Thing to Say?

There is no safer, more effective message to free up blocked emotional communication than to give empathy. Empathy is emotional salve. It heals wounds. The question "This is a hard time for you, isn't it?" is usually an excellent opening. When children feel truly, totally understood by you, they lower their defenses. They are less oppositional and much more open to what you have to say. Always start with empathy when talking with your child about any sensitive issue.

for the parent or other adult or giving up altogether the struggle to meet the adult's wishes. Then comes oppositional behavior.

Show empathy. It feels good to be understood. I have asked many parents to write that little maxim on a placard and place it on their bathroom mirror, so that each day they will remember to be truly empathic to their children's feelings.

Empathy paves the way for a bigger goal—true emotional intimacy with your child or teen. Intimacy means that both of you feel totally safe in revealing your deep-down honest feelings to each other. It also means that each of you knows that the other will respect your feelings and seek to find a win-win solution to any conflict that arises through the sharing of feelings.

Of course, there are some aspects of your life you don't share. It would be inappropriate, for example, to share your disappointment in a spouse with your child. But the overall goal here is to conduct the business of getting along without power struggles. Empathy helps your child feel safe in talking with you. Intimate conversation allows you to stand firm on important values while continuing to provide an open channel for your child to communicate with you.

Work Toward Joint Understanding

HOW THE TWO of you encourage or thwart emotional communication helps determine the strength of your relationship. You are not being intimate when you hide parts of yourself that *should* be shared and when you don't convey your true feelings or wants.

Of course, you can control only your half of your communication with your child. Even if your attempt is unsuccessful, you will have at least modeled the correct way to conduct an emotionally congruent sharing of feelings. You will have paved the way for better communication next time.

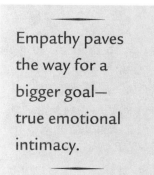

Empathy paves the way for a bigger goal— true emotional intimacy.

True relationship-healing intimacy consists of free, frequent, reciprocal exchange of relevant, emotionally significant information. Your job as the adult is to express information kindly, of course, but it also must be expressed truthfully, completely, clearly, and congruently. It must be expressed with impact, in an atmosphere of emotional safety. Let's take a closer look at each of these aspects of intimacy.

Intimate communication is free. Picture emotional intimacy between you and your child as somewhat similar to two containers of fluid connected with pipes. The fluid is emotionally significant information about your wants, hopes, needs, feelings, frustrations, and similar aspects of your relationship.

The liquid must flow—the exchange of information must occur.

Intimate communication is frequent. Infrequent communication forces each of you to take guesses at how the other feels and what the other would like—a dangerous process when the child already feels misunderstood. There is no reason why you can't attempt a daily intimate conversation with your child. The personal private interviews described in chapter 3 should take place at least every other week.

Intimate communication is reciprocal. Each of you should aim for self-revealing statements, and each should accept the other's self-revealing statements. In an ideal world, your child would make statements and would be accepting and kind about the statements you make. Given enough time, that will eventually happen. But your child is—by definition—immature, so as the adult, you're going to do more modeling of correct behavior, and you're going to be the recipient of more incorrect behavior. That's okay. Like teaching your child to ride a bike, teaching proper communication takes time and practice. No lecturing or preaching, please. Spend more time listening than talking.

Intimate communication is emotionally significant. Chitchat doesn't strengthen intimacy. It's superficial and often masks deeper issues. ("If I can engage Mom in a discussion about the weather, I'll distract her from wondering why I'm failing math." And similarly: "If I chatter on about the weather, I won't have to get into a discussion with John about why he's failing math.") Intimacy is strengthened through the discussion of important topics. Oppositional behavior is a signal that a topic is important and needs to be addressed.

Intimate communication is truthful. There's no intimacy if communication isn't honest. Holding back important facts and distorting information sabotages intimacy. Lying is a dangerous intimacy-destroying ploy of oppositional children and

Tell the Truth

Jeff was the son of a tough dad, a military type whose primary form of communication with his kids was the stern lecture. As a child, Jeff vowed he'd be a different sort of father.

But one day his seven-year-old son Adam was horsing around in the garage, and tipped Jeff's heavy toolbox onto the ground, chipping the concrete and barely missing Adam's foot. Angry at himself for leaving Adam unsupervised, scared at how very nearly Adam had been seriously injured—and perturbed about the chip out of the floor—Jeff lit into the boy. "What were you thinking?" he raged. "How many times have I told you . . ." The angry lecture went on for a full three minutes before Jeff slowed down long enough to draw breath . . . and then he saw Adam, head hung, shoulders slumped, trying to fight back the tears.

"I'm my father!" Jeff thought to himself, astonished. His own childhood resolution rang back in his ears. He stopped the lecture in midsentence, then knelt down beside Adam, hugged him, and apologized for losing his temper. "I was mad at myself for being careless and mad at you for almost hurting yourself. And I guess I'm mad that I have to fix the floor. Please don't ever climb on that toolbox again. Now let's hop in the car and go buy some stuff to patch up that hole."

teens. Follow the guidelines in chapter 5 about how to deal with lying.

Intimate communication is complete. It's often easier for parents—at least initially—simply to act on assumptions than to try to drag information out of an oppositional child. ("I don't know why she's being so cranky about going on this family vacation. It must be adolescent hormones. I'll just ignore it.") Sometimes, children and teens will avoid talking about a subject that appears to make their parents uncomfortable. While you might not agree with or approve of your child's emotional responses, it is still important that you understand his feelings about sensitive matters.

But don't act on assumptions about why your child behaves a certain way simply because she isn't easily approachable. Never assume you know the motives or feelings of another person. Motive guessing is often highly inaccurate. If your child isn't open and honest about the reasons behind difficult behaviors, don't simply forge ahead on your own assumptions. Instead, take an educated guess at what her real need or want is, then ask for confirmation about the accuracy of your guess. ("Jenny, it appears you're angry about going on this vacation. I'm guessing you're worried about being out of contact with your friends for two whole weeks. Am I seeing things correctly?")

> Like teaching your child to ride a bike, teaching proper communication takes time and practice.

Intimate communication is clear. Avoid vague statements. Never say "You ought to understand what I'm saying." Double-check the clarity of your communication by asking your child to repeat back to you what you have said, in different words from those you used. If your child can successfully paraphrase you, your communication has been clearly received.

Intimate communication is congruent. If your communication is congruent, the intent, content, and style all reflect the same underlying message. Body talk matches tone of voice, which matches the content of the message. Don't force your child to translate your meaning by sifting through a confusing mix of inconsistent body talk and words.

Watch your tone of voice because it is an especially powerful aspect of your communication with your child or teen. An overwhelming and sanctimonious tone of voice, a patronizing talking-down to your child, a bossy or dominating tone, an intimidating tone, and a sarcastic or critical tone of voice can all poison the process. Try using the same tone of voice you would use in talking with a cherished loved one 10 years older than your child. For example, if your child is 12, talk in a tone of voice you would use with a valued 22-year-old friend.

Try to keep corralling your child into congruence. When he is being manipulative or making a power play, he is being incongruent. Refuse to be drawn into his manipulation. Instead, invite him to state his genuine need and stay as congruent as you can.

> Listen carefully to your child's feelings, without discounting them or explaining them away.

Intimate communication has impact. If one person consistently takes the risk of revealing sincere feelings, but the other person never changes anything in response, the attempt at intimacy has not succeeded. Listen carefully to your child's or teen's feelings, without discounting them or explaining them away. Then show the benefit of this type of emotional honesty by making some changes in how things are handled or coming up with at least an attempt at a win-win solution.

Intimate communication includes emotional safety. A child or teen feels freer to share feelings if she knows she won't be judged, evaluated, or criticized for the thoughts and opinions that she shares. If the process of sharing is unsafe—in other words, if her efforts to communicate are met with sarcasm, ridicule, brush-offs, put-downs, one-upmanship, or inappropriate humor—then she'll quickly learn not to make the effort. Unfortunately for adults dealing with oppositional children, once that lesson's been learned, it's a difficult, time-consuming process to unteach it. If your child has learned that communication is unsafe, take a deep breath. Your task is clear: Make communication safe again.

Intimate communication reflects the total selves. Avoid understated, incompletely revealed messages that hide important relevant aspects of feelings. ("I'm a little surprised that you stole my new car and drove it into the lake." "Look who finally came home after being gone without explanation for three whole days. Could you take the garbage out?") Do your best to see that your child is also sharing thoughts about important issues that are relevant to his oppositionality, without holding back. Grunts, one-word responses, and evasive answers ("Somewhere." "Whatever!" "I don't know.") are blocks to human intimacy and require further investigation.

Tune In Totally

YOUR CHILD OR teen should feel free to share feelings with you without fear that you will look away, interpret his self-revealing as an attack, not pay attention, or give similar responses. An excellent place to start is to pretend to be a cartoon mouse with giant ears, two big eyes, and one very tiny and relatively silent mouth. Concentrate on listening and eye contact.

Assert your needs. The greatest challenges to your relationship with your child can occur when you are tired, emotionally drained, overwhelmed, angry, preoccupied with something, or in some other state of stress. Your actions during these times don't have to be negative. They can reflect a positive influence on your child and can model healthy handling of difficult situations.

A two-step guideline can turn emotionally stressful times into teaching moments. State (1) how you feel and (2) what you need in order to start feeling better. Announce that you are near the end of your rope and under great stress. Then state exactly and clearly what you want your child to do to help relieve the situation. In its simplest form, state what you want or need. For example:

1. How I feel: "I'm very tired now."

2. What I want: "I need to be alone for the next hour. I know it's your bedtime. Can you please put on one of your story tapes tonight? I'll come in and give you a good-night kiss in a few minutes."

Be ready to talk anytime. All living things need to be groomed and sharpened and given lots of care and attention. Family communication, trust, and respect are no different, and they require the same sort of nurturing. Misunderstanding and distrust increase as the amount of communication between the parents and children decreases. Being available to listen and to be with your children, especially when they need reassurance, can prevent an oppositional episode. Stop doing what you are doing—put down the paper, turn off the television, and listen. Practice being spontaneous and really tune in to your children's feelings without commenting on them. Remember, you're built with two ears and one mouth, not the other way around.

Try to respond to unpleasant feelings early in their development so that any difficulties are still small in nature. Waiting until your child or teen is having extreme emotional reactions to a situation makes finding a joint solution more difficult.

Expect differing points of view. To prevent oppositionality, try to bear in mind that the opinion or feeling being shared is probably your child's best effort at understanding and adapting to his situation. His emotions and beliefs are real, and they are developed through his own attempts to deal with the world and the people in it. Therefore, he has a right to have them and to express them in acceptable channels.

Listen with genuine regard and an open mind to what your child has to say. Your child must decide what his own values and beliefs are going to be, and he may make his point by contrasting his ideas with yours. Keep your eyes and ears wide open and your mouth closed during most of the conversation.

If there is an obvious clash of values, state that your point of view is different. Ask whether your child would like to know some additional information or an alternative viewpoint, then give it if invited. If your child says no, state that he must decide for himself and that you are always willing to discuss the matter further.

Convey feelings without distortion. A common error is to communicate to a child in terms that either understate the situation (too indirect and vague) or overstate it (too loud, too angry, too demanding). To state feelings honestly, use the four Cs. Your communication with your child should be:

- **Clear.** Do you state your feelings in a clear and explicit manner? ("I was really worried when you didn't come home by midnight. I thought you'd been in an accident.")

- **Calm.** Despite your feelings, are you able to control your temper, avoid making threats, and moderate your voice? ("Help me understand why you didn't call.")

Encouraging Healthy Emotional Communication

Avoid these roles that discourage your child from expressing beliefs and feelings honestly. Show acceptance by listening for feelings.

Role	Adult's Goal	Adult's Action
Commander	Keep things under control	Demand, order
Moralist	Child has "proper" feelings	Preach, "shoulds"
Know-it-all	Child is impressed	Lecture, advise
Judge	Adult is proved "right"	Assume child's guilt
Critic	Adult is proved superior	Ridicule, sarcasm
Shrink	Set the child straight	Interrogate, analyze
Fairy godparent	Excuse irresponsibility	Pretend all is well
Police officer	Child is never trusted	Doubt, snoop

- **Complete.** Is your communication bidirectional? Are both parties able to disclose and understand one another's disclosures? ("Let me see if I understand what you've told me. You didn't call because . . .")

- **Congruent.** When you feel confused, do you *look* confused? Do your words match your emotions? ("I need a better explanation.")

Sending emotional information clearly does *not* mean being "emotional." It means clearly describing how you feel and why. State your feelings by beginning a sentence with the phrase "I'm feeling" or "I feel."

Send congruent, understandable, accurate, and complete emotional messages. Your responsibility is to communicate in a reasonable way so that your child can interpret in a reasonable way. Don't simply announce "You ought to know how I feel." To be sure you have communicated clearly, ask your child to repeat back your meaning in general terms, rather than word-for-word parroting of what you just said. Work together at getting the messages understood.

By the same token, when your child communicates feelings, don't "respond" to his message. ("Oh, you shouldn't feel that way. That's silly.") Instead, paraphrase it and check to be sure you have understood it correctly. ("You're feeling anxious about being in a group of strangers, and you're not sure how to handle yourself. And you're angry at me for putting you in that situation. Am I understanding you correctly?")

By receiving a clear statement of your feelings and needs, your child is in a better position to be of genuine help and to respond in a caring manner. Communicating your needs in any other way opens up several harmful possibilities, including generating greater oppositionality in your child.

Avoid excess niceness. Some parents try so hard to sugar-coat negative feelings, hostility, disappointments, or conflict that their children never find out how those parents feel or what they want. The parent who tries to be unreasonably nice, polite, cheerful, and syrupy sweet at all times is throwing up a thick smoke screen that hides real emotions and feelings.

There is no such thing as a "bad" feeling; there are only bad actions. A bad feeling can be quashed, but it eventually degenerates into brooding, hostile, or obsessional thinking, which results in open hostility, anger, opposition, defiance, and a host of other dysfunctional behavior. Unpleasant feelings are like the warning lights on car or truck dashboards—they indicate that something is wrong. To correct the situation, give unpleasant feelings serious attention.

> There is no such thing as a "bad" feeling; there are only bad actions.

In general, people who respond to negatives with self-soothing thinking have healthier relationships than those who respond to negative emotions with hostile, escalating thoughts.

Help Your Child Understand and Clarify Feelings

POWER-ORIENTED MISBEHAVIOR is simply a form of self-expression. To prevent oppositional behavior, provide a clear channel for your child to express wants without misbehaving.

Help label feelings. If you sense that your child is having difficulty identifying the feeling or want, suggest different labels. For example, if your child claims to feel "bad" about how something went, seek clarification. Was it embarrassment? Frustration? Disappointment? Another way to focus on a feeling is to ask your child what he would like to do next in order to feel better. If he suggests an inappropriate action, ask "What would be a win-win thing you could do?"

Teach assertion of needs. A key step in negotiating for what we want in life is to help others know how we feel and what we need. Teaching this lesson to your child is a lifelong gift that will assist in all the relationships he will ever experience. Your child

needs to learn how to negotiate for what he wants, rather than acting out noncompliance, sneakiness, and oppositionality.

Urge the four Cs. To help assure that your child will be listened to and helpfully responded to, teach him how to express feelings using the four Cs.

Suppose, for example, that your teen is frustrated because of not getting to stay out as late as he would like in the evenings. A direct statement to you about that frustration holds more promise of relief than overstatement (loud complaining, swearing, whining, or a tantrum) or understatement (suffering in silence and never mentioning the need to you, becoming depressed). Ask your child to tell you what the concern is and to do so in the same fashion you are trying to model: clearly, calmly, completely, and congruently.

Only when you have received a four-Cs communication are you in a position to be of effective help at coming up with a win-win solution. There will be no need for defiant oppositional misbehavior.

Make Communication Safe and Profitable

WHEN CHILDREN BELIEVE communicating is not safe or profitable, they express their needs in incongruent ways, including becoming noncompliant and oppositional. Children believe talking isn't *safe* if adults dismiss their concerns as unimportant, criticize them, or violate in other ways any of the principles of communication in this chapter. They believe it won't be *profitable* if parents just pretend to listen, appear indifferent, change the subject, give false promises, or commit similar acts of sabotage against following through.

> When children feel communicating is not safe or profitable, they become noncompliant and oppositional.

Change the routines. To make sure that your child's attempts to communicate with you are profitable, listen attentively and respectfully. Help your child understand the feeling. Then, if it seems appropriate, offer loving support such as hugging, holding, or sitting with your child.

Demonstrate to your child that self-expression has impact by taking some steps to change the structure of things that disturb your child. Structural change means removing obstacles and finding alternatives. If two children who share a bedroom often argue and fight over who is throwing the dirty clothes on the floor, a structural solution would be a large hamper located inside the bedroom. If two children often argue over which television programs to watch, a structural solution would be a list of programs each child will watch from the weekly television program guide.

Always make some gesture. Whenever the answer must be no, try to move at least somewhat in the direction of resolving your child's difficulties. Your response to your child's concern doesn't necessarily include all the changes he wants, but some good should still occur from the conversation. Suppose your child expresses a desire to shoot hoops or read with you in the evenings. Your other obligations might make *every* evening impossible, but perhaps you are able to spend half an hour two times a week. And if even that much is impossible, your child deserves at least a full and loving explanation of why you're unable to grant his request.

Oppositional children tend to make requests in a manner that puts off their parents or other adults. They don't ask "Would you mind spending more time with me?" Instead, they accuse and demand: "All you care about is work. You're so selfish. You *never* do anything with me." It takes superhuman self-control to comply with requests when they're made in a hostile or aggressive manner. Keep reminding yourself that you and your child are not peers and that, as the adult, you're the one responsible for modeling correct behavior. Respond to hostility in a kindly manner, gently correct the hostility, and make explanations and adjustments anyway. Reassured of your love and having a new understanding that increased evening play is not currently available, your child is likely to feel far less frustration than if you had handled the issue less openly. Even though there is little increase in time spent together, both of you can be more at peace with this aspect of your relationship.

Showing your child that it is safe and profitable to assert personal needs doesn't mean stopping your leadership, nor does it mean letting your child become a tyrant by turning whims into demands. It does mean listening, answering honestly, showing basic respect, being alert to make changes in your routines, and encouraging your child.

You will prevent a considerable amount of opposition and defiance by keeping the channels for emotional communication clear and open. When an oppositional misbehavior occurs, however, you must deal with it. The first step is to confront your child or teen about the issue. Chapter 5 gives detailed guidelines for effective confronting to prevent further buildup of oppositional tendencies.

5

Confront Power-Oriented Misbehavior

W HY BOTHER WITH a whole book full of ideas
about how to get along with an oppositional, defiant
child? At first glance, it would seem an easy enough matter
simply to order the child to cooperate based solely on your authority as the parent, teacher, or other caretaking adult.
Unfortunately, things don't work that way. It would be nice if
they did.

Trying to overwhelm a resistant, defiant child with your
authority stimulates a backlash of pure rebellion. You can,
however, add other tools to your relationship skill tool kit.
Supplement your natural legitimate authority so that it becomes a contributing factor in the total influence you have on
your child. Throughout this book, I provide hundreds of ways
for you to gain more leverage with an oppositional, power-oriented child. Your authority should be part of the picture, but
don't try to make it the whole picture.

In this chapter, I address ways in which authority can be misused and describe its proper use in working with any oppositional child.

Avoid the Ignore-Nag-Yell-Punish Cycle

THE MOST COMMON pattern of inefficient adult response to misbehavior is the sequence of ignore-nag-yell-punish. None of these four steps is effective in stopping defiant, power-oriented misbehavior.

Stop ignoring. Far oversold as a discipline alternative by writers of parenting and counseling books, ignoring is one of the worst responses to a power-oriented child. Ignoring takes you out of the leadership role, risks omitting key aspects of supervision of your child, and sets no limits on your child's antics. Usually, your child will interpret ignoring as either a license to do whatever it was that she was trying to do in the first place or an invitation to keep badgering you.

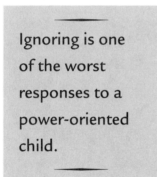

Ignoring is one of the worst responses to a power-oriented child.

Stop nagging. Piling words upon more words doesn't solve anything. In fact, the less you say, the better. Jabbering parents are weak and ineffectual and are prime targets for oppositional children. Telling a child five times to do something is not effective parenting.

Stop yelling. If raising your voice solved problems related to oppositionality, you wouldn't need a book like this. Oppositionality would have disappeared from the face of the earth long ago. Yelling implies all the wrong things and carries all the wrong messages to your child, not the least of which is that you don't respect her. If you don't respect her, you don't respect her wants. She will conlude that her only alternative then is to rev up and become even more oppositional.

Stop punishing. Punishment is an ineffective tool at best and a dangerous one most of the time. It doesn't build conscience; it sets you up to violate the child; it obligates you to inflict pain on your child; and it has many other negative features described in more detail in chapter 6. I have found that parents who rely on punishment to carry the discipline load tend to get deeply embroiled in vicious, lengthy power struggles with their children. These struggles often deteriorate into revenge deadlocks between parent and child.

Stop having tantrums. A typical ineffectual confrontation involves an angry parent who belittles and scolds in a harsh tone of voice, perhaps using abusive language. Physical attacks in the form of hitting, slapping, or spanking are often part of the scene, as are various deprivations and punishments. I call this type of confronting the "parent tantrum" method. My hope is that you will never again resort to it after you have read this chapter and the one that follows.

Don't Imitate Congress

BY THE TIME legislation has passed through the endless compromises of Congress, it is often so watered down in content, so tardy in delivering help, and so sabotaged by irrelevant amendments and attached conditions that it is of little effect. Don't let your attempts to solve oppositionality suffer the same fate. Stop indecision and "do-nothing" policies. You must actually do the work of confronting your child about disruptive, power-oriented misbehavior.

When children misbehave, they need to know that others are displeased. This knowledge is how they develop a conscience and how they take responsibility for the impact of their choices on the world around them. Your negative response is the natural consequence from which your child can learn important lessons.

In this section, I will use the word "confrontation"—a word that normally has negative connotations—to discuss the problem-solving conversations you have with your oppositional child. In this case, however, confrontation doesn't mean attacking one another, engaging in hostilities, or making war on each other. Picture instead a confrontation where the two of you are on the same side, and your mutual enemy is the "problem." Together, you're going to confront the problem (not each other), and you're going to attack it, fix it, resolve it, and make it go away.

It is important to present negative feedback in a positive way. Giving negative information doesn't mean you have to be unkind. How can you give an instructive, helpful, "negative" response?

Introduce the confrontation. I have found that getting children and teens to become less argumentative and less prone to power struggles works better if the conversations they have with adults are perceived as special events. As the adult, the best way for you to introduce confrontations is to state that you have some important things to discuss and don't want any interruptions or misunderstandings. Try to avoid answering questions about the upcoming conversation and keep the intent and content of it as vague and nondescript as possible. The ideal confrontation comes without giving your child a chance to rehearse a rebuttal.

Use a special location. For other than a brief everyday kind of confronting, use a special well-chosen location. You want to create some amount of concern or tension, without overdoing it. Taking your child out of the day-to-day environment deprives her of tension-relieving distractions. It means there are "no places to hide," so she must face whatever the issues are. One of the best locations is the front seat of your car in the parking lot of your child's favorite take-out restaurant. As your child is wolfing down her favorite food, start confronting. Some parents have found that inside a restaurant works, though I think such a setting can backfire on you because your child can easily make a very embarrassing public spectacle out of the conversation.

Some parents arrange an overnight in a motel. They can mix a pleasurable outing with the business of having a heart-to-heart talk. That method works excellently and is probably the best one but is a bit expensive.

Announce avoidance of the three Cs. In counseling with hundreds of oppositional, defensive, and defiant children and teens, I have developed a simple, effective way to introduce my role. I teach this technique to other mental health professionals as I travel throughout the United States and Canada giving training seminars on ODD. Any parent can use this same method.

Very early on, state that you're not going to do any of the three Cs to your child. You aren't going to criticize, control, or change her.

1. No criticism. Your purpose is to find win-win solutions, not attack your child. Your mission is to uplift and assist, not to push your child down. Your motive is love, not vindication.

> Very early on, state that you're not going to criticize, control, or change your child.

2. No control. You aren't going to boss or order your child around. Your goal is to find a win-win solution to the circumstance, and the only way to accomplish that goal is by shared problem solving in a two-way cooperative conversation with her.

3. No changing. You aren't going to attempt to change or manipulate your child. Any alterations in her actions as a result of your confrontation will be because *she* decided she wanted to make them.

Announce your three true goals. Your confrontation has three main purposes. They differ markedly from the three Cs. These goals are to:

1. Understand. Your goal is to learn exactly how your child feels. You are there to learn from her, to gain insight into how she sees things, and to find out what her needs are, what her opinion is, and how best to assist her.

2. Inform. You intend to let your child know how her actions are impacting other people in a negative way and, in turn, how she is also being hurt (or will be hurt in the future) by those actions. In other words, your goal is to give feedback on the results of her unacceptable actions, on others as well as on herself.

3. Help. You want to find solutions to assure that your child's needs do in fact get met. The solutions you want to develop are of the win-win variety. That fact means those needs will continue to be better met in the future because others will be more supportive than they have been up until this conversation.

Introduce the love motive. State that the only reason you are having this conversation is that you care very much about the welfare of your child. Your motive is a benevolent one based on love. For example, "My love for you causes me to express these concerns." Another useful way to express this concept is "I love you, or I wouldn't be mentioning this. I'd just let you suffer the results. But I do love you and want to help find a win-win solution."

Use the "I have a dilemma" approach. Introducing your confrontation with "I have a dilemma" arouses the interest of your child and paves the way for your child to be more receptive and less defensive. Writing this little speech down and handing it to your child as a love note is a very powerful way to confront. Say or write words that fit this format:

- **Introduce the dilemma.** "I have a dilemma. I have some concerns about you and your happiness. I love you very much, and my love and caring for you cause me to have these concerns. My dilemma is that if I *don't* tell them to you, I'm not giving you the benefit of my experience, my knowledge, and my love and caring for you. On the other hand, if I *do* tell them to you, I have fear."

- **State the fear.** "My fear is that you might not listen, will get angry, think I'm just preaching at you, or think that all I'm doing is criticizing or picking on you or telling you what to do."

- **Defend against the fear.** "I want you to know right off the bat that I'm not trying to criticize, blame, scold, control, boss, or manipulate you."

- **Proclaim your love motive.** "My love for you causes me to have these concerns. If I didn't love you, I wouldn't risk having this conversation. The fact that I'm willing to risk turning you against me by telling this to you shows how important these concerns are to me."

Proceed with the five-part confrontation procedure. Once you have introduced your confrontation, start into part 1 of the five-part universal confrontation procedure described later in this chapter. Give a description of the countable, observable actions that are of concern. Continue through the five parts, then obtain your child's response. One way to invite that response is to say something such as, "I have no way of knowing how you feel about this matter unless I discuss it with you like this. Do you have a similar concern to mine about the possible consequences of what you are doing?"

Get a "ticket to talk." For a very contrary child who simply won't listen, I have developed a special "deal" that sometimes bridges the gap. I call it the ticket-to-talk method. Introduce it as a way for your child to feel less nagged at by you. The deal is that you agree to give no more than three sentences of instruction or correction. In exchange for being relieved of "lectures," your child agrees to "really listen" and take to heart what you are saying. Although it is not the best parent-child communication, it is useful to prevent a deadlock and keep some communication flowing.

> For a very contrary child who simply won't listen, a special "deal" sometimes bridges the gap.

If you can't get a ticket to talk, your communication problems are severe enough to require the assistance of a skilled counselor.

Use the Five-Part Confrontation Procedure

THERE IS A universal way in which anybody can confront anybody else in a safe, effective way. Its power goes far beyond helping parents confront oppositional children and teens. I've used it to help couples renegotiate their stressed relationships and have seen it help employees confront their bosses—and vice versa.

For the purpose of improving your relationship with a power-oriented child, this procedure is ideal. It consists of five phases or steps to be accomplished in an exact order. In the example I will use, let's suppose your teen is being selfish and inconsiderate toward her younger brother.

Part 1. What you are doing. Describe in detail exactly what the quantifiable, observable actions are. Avoid vague impressionistic accusations such as "being a snot" or "making trouble." Be specific, objective, and nonjudgmental in your description. In our example, you might say: "This is the third time Andy has come to me in tears this week over something you have said to him."

The event is scientifically verifiable, observable, and countable. An incorrect attempt would be: "This is the third time you've had a bad attitude."

Part 2. How I feel when you do it. State the negative emotional reactions you experience when you hear of the misbehavior. It is admissible to acknowledge your knee-jerk reactions of anger, frustration, and disappointment. But quickly go underneath to the feelings that have more to do with your caring about the child. The real power in this step comes from reminding the child of those caring feelings, not from your indignation.

In our example, you might say: "When he comes to me like that, my first reaction is to get really angry with you. But then I stop and think about it, and what's more important is that I'm worried about what's happening to your relationship with him. You must be experiencing some horrendous stress in your life right now. I know you can't be happy when you act like that to your brother, and I want to find some ways to help you. I also worry about your brother's feelings of betrayal and hurt from you, and whether those will seriously harm how he gets along with you later on."

Notice that there is a certain point-blank honesty here, but it is not an attack on the offending child. You can get away with direct labeling of very negative feelings as long as you are simply straightforward and honest about it.

Part 3. What I want you to do differently. This part consists of two steps: what I want you to *stop* doing and what I want you to *start* doing instead. The request should consist of specific actions, not vague processes such as "change your attitude" or "shape up." Notice that it involves both starting and stopping—stop the undesirable action and start an acceptable replacement action. Notice also that this part is not denying the child the right to have a negatively experienced feeling. It merely provides a safer outlet for the feeling.

In our example, you might say: "I want you not to say cruel and offensive things to your brother anymore. No more swearing or calling him names. Whenever you feel irritable, tired, grumpy, or angry at your brother, I want you to come to me and tell me about it. You can simply give me a code statement like 'red flag' if you want to."

Notice that you are giving your teen the license to feel the unpleasant feeling but are aiming the *action* into an acceptable direction. Code words are helpful because they allow your child to transfer a need into a constructive assertion. Being assertive is what oppositionality is all about.

Part 4. How I will support those changes. State what you will do to meet your child halfway and bring support for both the stopping and the starting.

In our example, you might say: "If you stop saying cruel things to your brother, I'll work with you to get him to stop acting in ways that bug you. And if you come to me when you're feeling out of sorts, I'll stop doing whatever I'm doing and try to help you find a win-win solution to how you're feeling, so you won't have to resort to dumping your anger on your brother."

Notice that you don't do everything for your teen but are supportive of the action you are asking her to take. She has to assume some responsibility for making the new plan work. What you offer to do should be directly relevant to the conflict situation. Don't simply throw irrelevant rewards and enticements at your child. An example of an incorrect version of this part would be: "If you'll stop being mean to your brother, I'll give you a new CD and let you watch more television."

Part 5. Check in. Double-check each of the preceding four parts.

For part 1, does your child agree with you that the misbehavior has in fact occurred as you described? If you confined your statement of part 1 to countable and observable actions, there is little room for debate.

If, in fact, your child disagrees and claims, for example, that she didn't say anything cruel, the next step is to conduct a survey. Interview the brother and come up with a definition for a cruel statement, then count all instances during a specific period of time in the immediate future.

For part 2, does your child understand how you feel, both at the surface knee-jerk level (frustration) and underneath (concern about both children)?

For part 3, does your child understand exactly what you want stopped and what you want the new replacement actions to be? Again, you can see the importance of staying specific and countable in action descriptions, rather than vague. It's tough to agree on whether *attitude* has changed but easy to agree on whether *actions* have changed.

For part 4, does your child understand what specific help you are willing to provide and under what conditions? Is she willing to go along with this arrangement, at least experimentally, for a week or so?

> It's tough to agree on whether *attitude* has changed but easy to agree on whether *actions* have changed.

In our example, you might say: "Do you agree that three times last week you called him those offensive names and swore at him? Do you understand why I'm concerned about this? Do you understand what I want you to stop doing and to start doing instead? Do you understand the deal I'm offering you in support of these changes? Are you willing to go along with this plan?"

Obtain an answer to each question before proceeding to the next. The check in proves the reciprocity of this method because you are not taking any steps until you are sure your child is in full agreement all the way along. You are suggesting a genuine win-win solution and even offering to help make it happen. What a powerful, wonderful way to prevent silly power struggles and oppositional defiance!

Give Therapeutic Affection

THERE IS A very powerful procedure for confronting children and teens on-the-spot when you can't arrange an isolated meeting ahead of time to discuss things. This method keeps them calm and keeps the adults calm. I call it the therapeutic affection method. The basic idea is that you don't criticize your child but instead provide love on several simultaneous dimensions. The child stays much more calm and amenable to your corrective feedback than in the typical scolding type of confrontation. You are going to give Love TEA.

Touch. T stands for touch. Rub your child's back, touch him on the shoulder, or provide any other tender expression of touch-based affection he will accept. Sit as near to the child as you can and maintain eye contact. If your child won't accept any touch, simply move on to E.

Empathy. E stands for empathy, which involves four steps in my Love TEA procedure. Those steps can be represented by the first four letters of the alphabet:

- **A—Attend to your child.** Tune in, with two big eyes, two big ears, and one tiny mouth. You can't tune in if you're at the computer, watching television, talking on a cell phone, or dealing with something that is burning on the stove. Set all other concerns aside. Don't attempt therapeutic affection until you can attend in this fashion. You don't say anything about step A but simply position yourself near the child and tune in.

> All misbehavior reflects unmet needs.

- **B—Blanket empathy statement.** The statement that covers just about any situation like a warm blanket is "This is a hard time for you, isn't it?" These should be the first words out of your mouth during a Love TEA conversation.

- **C—Closed option motive guessing.** All misbehavior reflects unmet needs. Take educated guesses at the underlying needs your child was trying to meet by the misbehavior. Hunt for a yes or no answer to your guesses.

    For example, ask questions like "Did you do that because you want us to notice you more? You thought you should have more say about that? You wanted to get back at your sister for what happened Tuesday? You're starting to feel overwhelmed by these demands from your teacher? You wanted to see what would happen?"

Notice that you must take your child's point of view, not simply brand the motive in negative judgmental terms such as laziness, irresponsibility, or stupidity.

- **D—Demonstrate your understanding.** Prove that you understand by rewording your child's statements and checking for accuracy. For example, "Are you saying that you felt hurt by what your sister said so that's why you took both of her sweaters out of the closet?" Your ability to reword your child's feelings is proof positive that you understand.

Affirmation. The A in the Love TEA stands for affirmation. Affirm your caring and love and indicate that you empathize with your child's felt psychological pain. Also affirm that you wish better things for your child in the future.

Children often misinterpret "We don't like what you just did" as "We don't like you." The affirmation part of the Love TEA conversation prevents this kind of reaction from your child. In the affirmation phase, convey that you understand the painful feelings leading to the misbehavior and don't wish upon your child any such pain. You hope your child can become happy, feel safer, be contented, and so forth. For example, you might say: "We don't want you to feel unsafe around your sister, and we certainly don't want you to feel as if you have to be taking her things in order to protect your own privacy. We love you and appreciate you."

The affirmation is not praise, and it is not phony. It says you consider your child to be special and precious and that you don't want her to be burdened with the psychological pain that served as the underlying motivation for the misbehavior.

Get Around Smoke Screens

WHEN CONFRONTING A child about a potential conflict, you might be greeted with an interesting phenomenon. Your child or teen is going to act like a squid.

When a squid senses a predator, it squirts a dark fluid that confuses the predator. Meanwhile, the squid darts out of harm's way. In the same manner, your child may try to confuse you and try to get you to stop your attempt at confronting. The oppositional child's favorite forms of smoke screening parents are "I don't know" and "I don't care" answers to confrontation questions. It is important that you proceed with the confrontation. Don't let yourself be sidetracked by the attempt to throw up a smoke screen. Usually, "I don't know" means "I don't want you to pursue this, and I don't want to have to *think* about this." "I don't care" usually means "I don't want you to pursue this, and I don't want to have to *feel* about this." Your response should have the attitude "Oh, yes, you *do* have to think or feel about this, and I *will* pursue this."

Your noncompliant response to your child's attempt to sidetrack you should not actually involve those exact words. Here are six retorts, word-for-word, that I have found useful in getting past smoke screens from oppositional children and teens. Combine them as you use them to fit the circumstance:

1. "Let me re-ask that." Immediately ask the question again in slightly reworded form.

2. "We're just tossing around ideas here." This comment gives a relaxed, informal aspect to your conversation, lowering your child's defensiveness.

3. "You don't have to know; just take a guess." The child was connoting that since she didn't know, you should stop inquiring. This retort dismisses the fact that your child doesn't know as irrelevant and invites further thought.

4. "If you *did* know, what might it be?" This retort puts the child into hypothetical thinking mode, breaking the rigidity of denial.

5. "If you were hooked up to a lie detector and had to tell the truth, what would you say?" This retort is one of the most powerful. It works well with teens and adults. Like the preceding retort, it invites hypothetical thinking, which gets your child out of the position of rigid denial.

6. "Deep down inside, you *do* know." Your child can't refute this one because deep feelings are nondescript and not observable.

Label your child's defensiveness. Refer to defensiveness or a tendency to give smoke-screen answers as a mask that your child or teen is wearing. Then ask her to take off the mask so you can talk with the real person behind the mask. I have used this "externalizing" procedure very successfully with defiant, argumentative, and defensive children and teens. When externalizing, you are labeling the child's ploy as a thing—in this case, a mask—and asking her to do something with her ploy—in this case, set it aside.

You might say, for example, "Would you please take that teenager mask off, the one that makes you say: 'I shouldn't have to talk to you, and I don't want to be here'? I have some really important things I want to say to the real Cameron behind that mask." If your child or teen still resists, repeat your claim to avoid the three Cs, then proceed with the confrontation *as if* your child agreed to take the imaginary defensive mask off.

Use coleadership. The technique of coparenting or coteaching or coleadership prevents your child from manipulating you and playing one adult against the other. For example, suppose your child comes home from school and insists she has no homework. Yet the teacher had informed you previously that your child will have homework every single day. Which person should you believe—your child or the teacher? With coleadership, it's not an issue. You and the teacher might agree that if there's ever a time when your child has no homework, the teacher will provide a written note. Without the note, the child has homework. When your child faces two adults who are united in their position, she can't manipulate. (To help prevent homework-based power struggles, use the Taylor Classroom Daily Report Form, available free from A.D.D. Plus, P.O. Box 4326, Salem, OR 97302.)

When your child makes a request that merits a joint decision, arrange a delay until you can schedule a quick coleading decision-making conversation with the other parent, the teacher, or whichever other adult is party to attempted manipulations. During your coleadership conversation, come to a mutually agreed-upon answer for your child.

Now your child is facing a four-legged creature who says "We have decided that . . ." and is therefore much less likely to attempt further manipulations. Save this technique for those moments in which a simple quick decision from one adult is not sufficient or is likely to run up against opposition from the child.

Ask for more time. Impulsive answers to manipulative children get parents into trouble. Claim at least a few minutes of time to sort out the ramifications before providing an answer to your child's request. When you are the one initiating the conversation, think about exactly what you want before making a request of your child or teen.

Control yourself. A principle I have used for many years in my practice with families is "control yourself, not your child." Take your sails out of the wind of your child's invitation to have a power struggle with you. You can't prevent your child from sending out an invitation to struggle, but you can control your response to that invitation. There can be no victory if the opponent never shows up to battle. Say: "I'm not going to argue or power struggle with you about this. The only thing I'm willing to do is discuss it with you to find a win-win solution."

Observe the invitation to power struggle. Your child wants to experience strength illegitimately by opposing you. It is important that you recognize your child's attempts to lure you into a power ploy. If you refuse to enter the struggle, you sidetrack the power struggle. Determine that you will *observe*, but never enter, your child's power-struggle invitations.

> It is important that you recognize your child's attempts to lure you into a power ploy.

One way to avoid being drawn into a power struggle is to pretend you are a scientist. Have a detached attitude of looking through a one-way mirror and impartially observing your child's antics. Stay unmoved as you note body position and tone of voice.

Correct without criticizing. One of the principles I learned from family therapist Virginia Satir is that there is nothing inherent in a negative situation that means you must deal with it in a negative way. There are important differences between giving corrective feedback and conducting a verbal attack. You might ask how a parent can avoid being critical or negative in a situation in which the child is in the wrong. The answer is simple. Apply chapters 3 and 4 of this book as you confront your child about an incident of misbehavior.

Arrange pit stops and huddles. When auto racers pull into the pit, they *withdraw* from the contest, *assess* how they are doing, *renew* their vehicles with gas and replacement tires, then *re-enter* the race. These same steps—withdraw, assess, renew, re-enter—also apply to confronting a power-oriented child or

Are You Correcting or Criticizing?

Here is how to confront your child about misbehavior or poor decisions in a way that doesn't devastate self-esteem. Notice how many of the characteristics of criticizing send the child in the direction of becoming more oppositional.

Two Models of Communication

Effective (Confronting)	Ineffective (Criticizing)
Child is asked for opinion	Child is told what to think
There is two-way communication, equal sharing of feelings	Parties experience one-way communication
	Adult talks, child listens
Child has choices, considers options	Child has no choice, is told what to do
Child learns how to make decisions	There is no learning about decision making
Child's logic is discovered, clarified	Child's logic hidden, remains distorted
Leading questions are asked	Adult preaches, lectures
	Adult demands obedience
There is problem solving	Harmony is damaged
Adult promotes harmony	Adult demands that child adopt adult's point of view
Adult asks that child consider adult's point of view	
Parties resolve underlying issues leading to crisis	Basic issues, child's needs remain unresolved
Adult doesn't nag or repeat messages	Adult is nagging and wordy
Adult models values being taught—courtesy, kindness	Adult models demanding, bossy behavior

teen. Be willing to stop whatever you are doing and invite your child to join you in the pit stop. Assess the ongoing process between the two of you, come up with a better way of handling the situation, then re-enter the scene with the new, better method.

Suppose your teen has a very loud, foul mouth first thing in the morning. You ask for a pit stop and share the observation that she seems very angry and full of venom. She tells you why, and you empathize. Together, you come up with a win-win approach, and you invite her to re-enter the room with a more humane vocabulary.

Some adults have found that the code word "huddle" also works well, especially if the child understands the concept of a football huddle. Either person can ask for a huddle or pit stop. At times, your child may request one in order to express concern about something you are doing that is bothering her. This is a good example of a safe, user-friendly technique for dealing with defiance. This one works for just about any family or group and is especially helpful when oppositionality is an issue.

Try the sandwich technique. How do you make a sandwich? You put bread on the bottom, fill in the middle, and add more bread on top. In the same way, present unpleasant or hard-to-take information to your child in a sandwich: First some good news, then the bad news, then more good news. A sandwich style of confronting about towels on the bathroom floor, for example, would sound something like this: "I appreciate the fact that you are keeping yourself clean by daily showering. It would help a great deal, though, if you could please put your used towel into the hamper rather than leaving it in the middle of the floor. And thanks, honey, for taking the time to make the bathroom a little safer and tidier for whoever uses it next."

Give the pie-crust analogy. Refer to the behavior you wish your child would change as the dough from which a pie crust is made. Explain that the top crust of a pie is made by draping the crust over the filled pie shell, then trimming away the excess around the edges. You're not asking your child to become someone else or surrender her uniqueness. All you want is that your child make slight adjustments—trim off the useless part of her behavior.

Deal directly with lying. One of the most difficult roadblocks to honest communication with an oppositional or defiant child, lying prevents a frank discussion of what really happened. It also gives the child a great amount of illegitimate power because you can't make her tell the truth, and the lying can provide a cover-up for almost any kind of misdeed. Many oppositional children become so skilled at lying that they lose their awareness of what is real and what is fantasy. The various types and advantages of lying for the oppositional child were discussed in chapter 2. If your child lies to evade consequences or avoid a responsibility or chore, try these eight steps:

> Many oppositional children become so skilled at lying that they lose their awareness of what is real and what is fantasy.

1. **Discuss.** Avoid focusing on your child as a liar. Instead, highlight the lie and treat it as the topic. Discussing the lie helps put your child in a more objective, emotionally removed position. Explain that all lies are of three basic types: to claim to be more than you are, to claim to be less than you are, and to stir up excitement. Of course, there are additional motives among certain children who have severe personality or conscience disorders, but categorizing lies into these three groupings will work in the vast majority of instances. You might

explain: "Some lies say you are more than you are, like bragging about something you have or something you did. Other lies say you are less than you are, like saying you didn't do something wrong or didn't take something that belonged to someone else. And some lies are just to stir up excitement and get people all upset. Which type of lie was this?"

Try to remain as scientific and analytical as you can, avoiding emotionality. Notice that you are focusing on the lie, not on the child. Explore the thoughts that led to your child's lie. Get her to state her motives and intentions behind the lie—what she was trying to accomplish or avoid.

2. Empathize. Make it safe emotionally for your child to convey these feelings to you by showing empathy. Show your understanding of whatever need your child was trying to meet by telling the lie. Feel no obligation to identify with "being a liar," but do try to find some common ground with your child in terms of the underlying neediness that provoked dishonesty.

Suppose, for example, that your child claims not to have been a part of group vandalism in which she actually did participate. Show that you have had experiences, or could at least imagine having experiences, involving a fear of being caught at something. You aren't endorsing the act of vandalism or the act of lying, but you are building an emotional connection with your child.

3. Label the mistakes. Having shown empathy for your child's logic and motives, label them as mistakes. If the lying occurred as a cover-up for a misdeed, two mistakes have occurred: the misbehavior itself and the cover-up attempt. In our example, you might say: "You made two mistakes here. The first was thinking the best way to make the other kids like you was to join them in spraying the paint on the building. The second was to think you needed to lie and deny what you did."

4. Introduce the negative impact. Gently explain the undesirable domino effects of each mistake. These effects are actually natural consequences, described in detail in chapter 6. Talk about the future, not the past. In our example, you might say: "Now it will be harder for those kids to like you, rather than easier. You tell me why." (The child responds.) "And it will be harder for you to make friends with the kids who don't get into trouble. Why is that?" (The child responds.) "And it will also be harder for me to trust you. Why?"

5. Explain negative consequences. Once you have cracked the ice, proceed with outlining the natural consequences of developing a reputation as an untrustworthy person who lies. Include the ideas that people will learn not to trust her, a reputation as a liar will be hard to change, people will stop telling her their secrets, and so forth. Keep this and the preceding explanation in simple, concrete terms with a clear cause-and-effect sequence.

6. Explore the consequences of truthfulness. Discuss the positive, natural results of becoming honest about this matter. Focus on the impact on other people and their feelings. They will be more likely to bring her into their confidence, treat her with greater respect, and so forth.

7. Encourage apology. Review the Eight A's of Apology (discussed in chapter 6) to clear up any damaged feelings or relationships over the incident.

8. Get a commitment for change. Help your child think of what to change for next time. Arrange that in return for an agreement not to lie about future incidents, only logical consequences will apply, that is, simple compensation or repayment.

Get warmth before confronting. One of the most potent of the techniques I use to heal families in which oppositional misbehavior and power struggles have been occurring is the thermometer principle. Simply stated, it means that the parent imagines a giant thermometer that, instead of temperature, measures the degree of emotional closeness a child feels toward the parent. The thermometer is horizontal, as if lying on the floor.

The parent is at the base of the thermometer, at the tip of the warm side. The child is at the other end, at the tip of the cold side. When there is conflict, the child feels emotionally distant from the parent or cold toward the parent. The parent also senses this emotional distance.

The thermometer principle is that you must pull the child onto the warm side of the thermometer before you can successfully confront him about a conflict or misbehavior incident. Note that this principle reflects the *opposite* of what most parents do when their children misbehave.

I have discovered four highly effective approaches by which a parent can get a child or teen to become more mellow and willing to negotiate a win-win solution to potential conflicts. You might consider these as ways to lure your child onto the warm side of the thermometer:

1. **Empathy for the pain.** As you know from reading previous chapters, empathy is the best emotional salve in the

world. Instead of scolding for the misbehavior, empathize with the pain underneath it. Ask yourself, "Have I ever been in a situation in which I felt that way?" Hopefully the answer is yes or that at least you could imagine how your child must feel.

Prove you understand; don't just claim you understand. Suppose, for example, the misbehavior is not doing homework. Have you ever been in a situation in which something you were supposed to do was totally repulsive to you and you just couldn't bring yourself to face it? If the answer is yes, then say: "I know how it feels to have to do something that you find very unpleasant and just don't have the energy for. I remember one time on my job . . ." Great! You have your child's undivided attention, and your child is inching toward the warm side of the thermometer as you speak.

2. Appreciations. Give genuine statements of appreciation and gratitude for various aspects of your child's character and behavior. Are there traits that you admire and respect? Does your child have characteristics you wish you had more of? Can you genuinely thank him for something? I hope so. The appreciations help move your child along toward the warm side and away from an entrenched "I don't like you, and I want what I what when I want it" position at the opposite end of the thermometer. Under the warmth of your affirmations, your child's rigid resistance will melt.

In our example, you might say, "I appreciate the way you act so responsible about taking care of your pets and doing your violin lessons. And I'm so glad you enjoy your babysitting and your work with the scouts."

3. Common ground. Point out the similarities you and your child share by virtue of your traits as well as your experiences. Try to stay as relevant to the situation at hand as you can. In our example, you might say: "You and I are alike in that we both tend to bite off more than we can chew sometimes.

I know at the office I'll take on projects that I should delegate, then push myself to meet deadlines that are too early. I think maybe you're doing the same thing here. Maybe it's time to take another look at how many things you have going to occupy your time and energy."

The effectiveness of this step in the thermometer conversation pivots on the ability of your child to see you as an ally rather than an adversary. Similarity automatically puts you in the same boat and gives you added credibility as you show your empathy for your child's feelings underlying the misbehavior. Your child continues to inch toward the warm side.

> Express faith and confidence that things can work out, that your child will be able to find happiness.

4. Hopes and dreams. Indicate your good wishes for the future of your relationship with your child as well as for your child's overall life experiences. Express faith and confidence that things can work out, that your child will be able to adjust better and find happiness. In our example, you might say: "I want us always to have a relationship in which you can feel free and safe to come to me and tell me whenever you are starting to feel overwhelmed or bothered. I love you very much and want nothing but the best for you." Your child continues toward the warm side of the thermometer.

Putting Confrontation into Action

ONCE YOU HAVE shared your empathy, appreciations, common ground, and hopes and dreams for your relationship, your child will no longer be stuck at the faraway end of the thermometer. Hopefully, your child will be on the warm side, feeling close to you and in contact with warm feelings about you and about relating to you. Now your child has room to back up while you confront. After you confront, there is still a good chance your child will be on the warm side of the thermometer. The closer your child feels to you at the beginning of this step, the greater the chance he will stay on the warm side.

Use the five-part universal confrontation procedure. In our example, you might say:

1. What you are doing. Be sure your assertion is countable and observable. "I need to talk with you about the phone call I got from the school counselor. She said you haven't turned in any homework in social studies, science, or math for the last week."

2. How I feel when you do it. "When I hear things like that, I start to feel very concerned that you are probably experiencing too much pressure and have too many things going on in your life right now. I also worry about the effect it will have on your grades and on your college applications."

3a. What I want you to stop doing. "I want you to stop getting discouraged, and I want you to stop hiding your school problems."

3b. What I want you to do instead. "Whenever you feel overwhelmed and burdened by school assignments, or anything else for that matter, I hope you will come and talk to me about it."

4. How I'm willing to support those changes. "If you do that, I'll be happy to inventory how we might be able to cut back on some of the other things we've been expecting you to do. I'll also be willing to go to your teachers and see if we can get them to reduce or delay some of those assignments while you get caught up."

5. **Check-in.** "Is it accurate to say that you haven't turned in the homework for a week? Do you understand how I feel about it? Do you understand what I'm offering to help you out of this predicament? Are you willing to come to me and talk about this and work to reduce the demands that are on you right now?"

The combination of the thermometer method and the five-part universal confrontation procedure is almost unbeatable. In fact, I've never known an instance in my years of family clinical practice in which this combination has failed to produce positive changes in deadlocked family power struggles.

Let's Make a Deal!

A STRATEGY I have used hundreds of times in counseling teens who struggle for power is to make deals with them. They suddenly sit up and take notice when I mention the magic word "deal," probably because they think they're going to get some leverage or advantage from it. The universal "deal" consists of two parts: what I want from you and what I'll give you in return. It helps to introduce the deal as a win-win proposal.

What I want from you. The first part is cooperation in some form or another. What you want is that your child stop misbehaving, do what is supposed to be done, change routines in the morning, stop badgering and pestering about something, and so forth. It should consist of specific, observable, countable actions—not attitude shifts or vague changes such as "shaping up."

What I'll do in return. The second part is that you will support that change in some way. The support you give should be relevant. I don't recommend dangling arbitrary rewards for behavior improvement because "behavior modification" schemes don't build conscience. The best they can do in most circumstances is improve compliance as long as the reinforcing adult is present, directly supervising, and giving out rewards at the time. Frankly, I don't care what your child does when an adult is standing over her and dishing out rewards. I want to know what your child does when nobody is looking. I want conscience, and I hope you do, too.

Suppose, for example, that your teen wants much more use of the family car than you think proper and suitable. You might say: "Let's make a deal so we can have a win-win solution. I can't afford the extra gas and maintenance expense that happens when you use the car to the extent that you want. Here's what I'm willing to do. If you will bring it back full every time you take it out and pay half the extra insurance we pay to list you as a driver, you can have the car for one outing each evening that it's not being used by us. Can you go along with that?"

Notice that the procedure is somewhat open-ended in that you are asking for a response or even a counteroffer. You are directly addressing and validating your teen's need for socializing and going places. You're not criticizing your teen for wanting to waste time or use up your gas. Your deal also takes into account your need to protect your finances. There is no scolding or lecturing, simply a straightforward proposal for a potential solution that takes into account everyone's needs.

Sidestep Power Struggle Invitations

INCORPORATE THE PRINCIPLES in this chapter into the fabric of day-to-day problem prevention within your family or group. Intervene early in all potential conflicts so no molehill grows into a mountain.

The best approach to power struggles is to avoid entering into them at all. Here is a collection of principles from this chapter that shows how you can sequence these strategies in the process of sidestepping the invitation to engage in a power struggle.

Isolate the conversation. "I have something special to discuss with you. Can we meet in the other room in five minutes?"

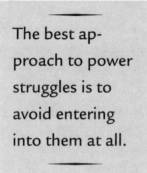

The best approach to power struggles is to avoid entering into them at all.

Remain nonjudgmental. If you have not actually caught the child at the misbehavior, don't accuse on circumstantial evidence. Say instead, "I don't know for sure whether you've done this, but I have a concern."

Acknowledge influence without total control. Ultimately, nobody controls anyone but himself. You might be able physically to force a small child to perform a task, but you can't control his willingness to comply or his attitude. And eventually, you'll even lose the struggle to force the compliant behavior. So don't even start down that path. If you're already on it, leave.

You want your children to control themselves. It's smart parenting to acknowledge that your child controls her own behavior while introducing your confrontation. "I don't control you and I don't want to." "I'm not handcuffed to you." "I have too much respect for you to try to make you . . ."

Start with the child's wants and needs. Your own needs are secondary to those of the person from whom you're seeking cooperation. So start there. Ask: "What can we do so that you'll want to . . . ?" "If you could determine how everything goes, what would you like to see happen?"

State your feelings clearly, completely, and honestly. Once your child sees that her needs are important to you, she'll be more open to hearing yours. "If you do it the way you say you want to, I would feel . . ." "Doing it entirely your way would create a problem for me."

Define the limits and conditions for your cooperation.
"Here's what I propose . . ." "I'll make you a deal . . ." "I won't
clean dirty ashtrays or clothes that smell of smoke."

Get permission to state your desire. "May I tell you what I
wish you would do about this matter?" "Would you like to
hear what I think would be best for you to do?"

Indicate your refusal to enter a power struggle. "I won't
power struggle with you about this." "I'm not going to try to
settle this with a shouting match." "I'm not going to argue
with you about this." "I want a peaceable solution, not more
conflict." "The only thing I'll settle for is a win-win solution."

State exactly what you wish your child would do. "What I
think would be best for everyone is that you . . ." "How about
if I do this and you do that . . . ?" "What I wish you would
choose to do is . . ."

Insist on a win-win solution. "The only solution I will accept is a win-win." "Power struggles and arguments are lose-
lose; I want a win-win for me and for you."

Keep the door open. "I want you to know that I'm always
willing to renegotiate." "Let's talk about this again tomorrow."
"Let's explore this issue some more when you're not so tired."

Put the emphasis on prevention, stay out of power struggles, and help your child use instances of misbehavior as learning moments for developing better decision-making skills and
a stronger conscience. Keep lines of communication open and
never lose sight of your overriding concern for your child's
well-being and of your love. By using this approach to child
discipline, you will maximize the likelihood of increased self-
control and better judgment.

The next chapter provides a framework for humane, sensitive, conscience-building discipline strategies if further misbehavior occurs.

6

Use Wise, Preventive Discipline

MANY PEOPLE EQUATE the word "discipline" with "punish." When asked what to do when their child argues or tries to launch a power struggle, most parents of oppositional children and teens give the knee-jerk response of "discipline the child." What they mean is punish the child. Yet truly effective discipline means seldom resorting to the so-called discipline techniques such as punishment.

Interestingly, the Latin root word for discipline reflects the idea of learning, not suffering.

> Truly effective discipline means seldom resorting to punishment.

Focus on Prevention

WITH OPPOSITIONAL CHILDREN, it is much better to prevent conflicts than to get out of ongoing conflicts.

Customary thinking about child discipline is excessively retroactive. The emphasis is on what to do *after* the misbehavior has occurred. Refocus your disciplinary efforts to proactively motivating your child toward desired behavior. Five key principles, all beginning with S, can help save your sanity if you live with a defiant, power-oriented child or teen:

1. Sufficient sleep. Inadequate sleep is one of the most controllable factors for preventing conflicts with oppositional children and teens. Although children vary in their need for sleep, most require 9 to 10 hours nightly. Elementary school students should get about 10 hours of sleep, and the ideal duration for teens is 9 to 10 hours.

2. Sufficient nutrition. Numerous research projects have demonstrated that a diet low in proteins and high in sugars and other carbohydrates pushes oppositional children and teens in the direction of worse behaviors: defiance, hostility, and physical aggressiveness. Other research has shown that lowering carbohydrates and sugars while providing increased protein, vitamins, and minerals tends to decrease rebellious misbehavior among teens who are in groups and other supervised situations.

3. Schedule need-meeting activities. All misbehavior reflects unmet needs. If you keep your child's needs met, misbehavior disappears.

One way to stay on track is to establish routines at every potential high-stress event—wake-ups, mealtimes, during chores, afterschool hours, and bedtime. Review daily routines at family meetings and post them on a small bulletin board or the refrigerator. Maintain the routines as much as possible. Explain why significant temporary changes in routine are necessary.

Establish additional routines that address your child's unique needs. Suppose that when your child became irritable and struggled for power, you discussed what was happening with him. He revealed that he is bored and lonely and doesn't have enough friends. He doesn't need lectures and punishments about being irritable. He needs improved social contacts. Routinely schedule some opportunities for upgrading his experiences with peers.

4. Structure to prevent problems. Preventing power struggles and other discipline problems requires the thoughtful placement of objects. Carefully place and arrange objects ahead of time to prevent problems from occurring.

Don't leave money on the dresser in an unlocked bedroom while you are away. Have schoolbooks in a special place so they won't be forgotten in the morning. Have cleaning supplies ready and available at chore time.

5. Supervise periodically. Some oppositional and defiant children tend to lie and to omit information if not asked directly for it. The net result is lowered trustworthiness. You might not feel able to believe what your child tells you, even though you wish you could.

During any activity, check periodically to make sure your child is proceeding correctly. This maneuver allows you to deal with problems while they are still small and manageable.

Use close supervision and don't rely simply on the honor system. Outline what you expect, then check for compliance. Clearly state behavior guidelines. Decide in advance how you and the child will both know when a rule is being observed or when it has been broken.

Suppose the rule is that homework must be completed, checked, and corrected before the TV is turned on. The method for enforcing the rule is to have your child bring the checked and corrected homework to you, then after you have examined it, you allow the television to be turned on

Support Your Child's Efforts

> Decide in advance how you and your child will know when a rule is being observed or when it has been broken.

TO ENSURE CONTINUED success, provide instruction on any changes needed next time and offer encouragement. For homework, follow the "three strikes and you're out" rule. Your child tries twice on difficult items, then comes to you for help if he still hasn't been able to find the answer. Your help is available at all times.

Give clear, nonwordy instructions. Make clear, concise, directive statements describing what you want your child to do. Consider that the ultimate responsibility for your successful communication to your child rests with you, not with your child. Use the principles of effective communication from chapter 5.

Use few words. Because the verbal channel is the most readily available for launching a power struggle invitation, stay out of it. Try not to steer or direct your child with words from far away. In general, keep the number of verbal directives low. Don't assume your child will understand and remember your message. Ask him to repeat it, if such a request does not cause conflict.

Use good "body talk." Approach your child so you can talk in a normal volume from a courteous distance. Stoop, kneel down, or sit facing a young child. Wait until he is quiet, obtain eye contact, then give your instructions in simple terms.

Again, don't assume your child will understand and remember your message. Ask him to repeat it, if such a request does not cause conflict.

Use Charts—Not Your Tongue

CHARTS KEEP YOU out of power struggles by providing constant reminders. They are silent and efficient substitutes for your memory and your tongue. Chart the steps your child is supposed to follow, using pictures if he is too young to read. I have found these four charts especially useful for families with difficult or defiant children.

The fun idea list. Boredom is one of the major contributors to misbehavior of oppositional children. This list can be extremely useful for preventing discipline problems. At the first feeling of boredom, your child can consult the fun idea list for something to do.

Invite your child to use the special phrase "I'm bored" whenever boredom sets in. I have found the "I'm bored" phrase very helpful in preventing arguments and misbehavior.

Let's Have Fun!

Look for detailed suggestions for the fun idea list and fun idea drawer in appendix A.

The few moments spent helping your child find something constructive to do pay off richly.

The fun idea list should be mounted low enough to be easily seen and should include various categories of activities: indoor and outdoor, quiet and active, alone and with other children. In a few minutes, you can come up with dozens of ideas, and you can supplement your list with ideas from library books on children's activities. Add new activities to the fun idea list as you think of them so that the list consistently matches your child's interests throughout the growing years.

The chore chart. Simple chore charts let each family member know instantly who is supposed to do what chore each day or week. Review chores at family meetings and post them on charts.

You have three variables to juggle: who, when, and which chores. Put one variable across the top, one down the side, and one in the middle of the matrix. For example, across the top appear six different chores, down the side are the seven days of the week, and in the middle of the matrix are the names of the family members.

The master chart. To decrease arguments and power struggles over homework and evening activities, use this chart. Make one for each quarter and mount it on a wall in your child's room to remind him of deadlines and appointments. Include all waking hours in large blocks of paper, with school-related tasks; long-term assignments; test dates; appointments; extracurricular programs, meetings, events, and activities; visits during the evenings and weekends; and similar information. Have your child pencil in class hours, mealtimes, travel times, work hours, and regular activities.

The daily activities chart. To help structure the day for a child who is going to be unsupervised for a period of time or who needs extra reminders, use this chart. Start with the skeleton of the day, divided into half-hour segments. Write down the proposed daily schedule on a large chart and mount it on the child's bedroom wall or closet door. Fill in the spaces with the activities for the day. Consider including coming home from school as well as household chores, afterschool snacks, homework, extracurricular activities, recreation, personal time, entertainment, socializing, mealtimes, and church or scout activities.

Here is a sample of the afternoon and evening portion of the daily chart activities:

3:00–3:30	Arrive home, snack, and rest
3:30–4:00	Homework
4:00–4:10	Break
4:10–4:50	Homework
4:50–5:10	Practice piano
5:10–6:00	Play outside
6:00–6:40	Dinner and cleanup
6:40–7:20	Homework and computer
7:20–7:30	Tidy room
7:30–8:40	Free time
8:40–8:50	Snack and brush teeth
8:50–9:00	Family prayer time
9:00–9:10	Final bedtime preparations
9:10	In bed, tuck-in, and tapes

Establish Workable Rules

TO AN OPPOSITIONAL child, rules were made to be argued about. You want your family's rules to be minimally challenged by a child who is power oriented. In order to ensure maximum cooperation with family rules, follow these guidelines.

The guardrail function of rules. Rules are like guardrails on a bridge. Traffic would proceed at a snail's pace across a high bridge on which there were no guardrails, but it moves quite rapidly if guardrails are present. Yet the lanes are the same width in both conditions. The presence of guardrails frees drivers up to proceed straight ahead on their journey, without having to slow down and check side to side constantly as they cross the bridge.

In the same way, rules and limits provide reassurance to the child so that he can proceed through his life journey without having to search for the edges. In other words, your child can't proceed through life unless there are rules and enforced limits on his behavior. Having orderly processes and reasonable rules within the family gives your child permission to experience strength in a healthy way. Like guardrails, rules should be on the edge, not in the middle of the lane. Let your child make most decisions about day-to-day living, thereby experiencing autonomy and self-direction. There will be little or no need for excessive power through oppositionality or defiance.

Make rules that are reasonable. Rules should make sense. If the child can't understand why something is necessary, there is less motivation to conform to it.

There should be a logical basis so that the child would come to the conclusion on his own that the rule would be a good idea.

Keep rules reasonably in tune with your child's age, judgment, memory, and activity level. Avoid restrictions or demands that extend beyond a reasonable range of a child's talents and tendencies. Don't have a rule, for example, excluding a child from ever listening to the radio or watching TV. Having rules that are tempting for a child to break is an open invitation to sneaky oppositionality followed by lying as a cover-up.

Make rules that are preventive. If an issue or event can't be decided at the moment and handled smoothly by the involved family members, you need a rule.

Fortunately, most interactions among family members require no rules, just common sense and courtesy. Keep rule making to a minimum. Make no more rules than you have to in order to ensure harmonious processes within your family.

Make rules that are fair. Unfairness to a power-oriented child is like a matador's flag to a bull. Fairness means that the rule "fits" the child as well as the situation. It doesn't mean treating everyone identically. Enforce with rules your efforts to emphasize the uniqueness of each child in your family. Suppose there are two older children and one infant in

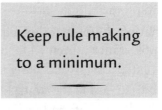

Keep rule making to a minimum.

the family. A rule that the big sister supervises her baby brother whenever the parents are away for a short period is not unfair if she is a better choice for infant care than her brother.

The relationship of fairness to sameness is discussed in chapter 7.

Make rules that are enforceable. Avoid restrictions or demands that can't be supervised or monitored in some way. Make only enforceable requests, such as "Don't take your brother's sweater without asking" rather than "Don't do anything that your brother doesn't like."

When supervision is minimal, post a chart listing the expected activities for which you have established your rule. In general, rules should govern physical actions, not thoughts, feelings, and attitudes. Actions can be observed, counted, and identified. Inner feelings can't.

Base rules on genuine need. The fewer rules, the better. In essence, a rule is a substitute for negotiation and on-the-spot sharing of mutual feelings and awarenesses between the people involved in the event. Rules are rather lame substitutes, too. A family with too many rules lacks healthy emotional transactions among its members. Only if certain routine events would otherwise create friction should there be a rule to govern those events. Confine rules to issues that really matter when health, safety, social learning, personal development, or key family processes are at stake.

Enforce the rules. You must maintain orderly processes within your family. Rules assist in that process, provided they fulfill the criteria just mentioned. Enforcing rules means monitoring to see whether they were observed and whether their observance prevented the problems they were intended to prevent. If they were observed, great! If not, confront the rule breaker, using the strategies given in chapter 5.

By definition, breaking a rule is misbehavior. But just because a rule was broken doesn't mean that the child must face a disciplinary consequence. What if the rule wasn't valid at that moment or an exception to the rule occurred? Rules can outgrow their usefulness at any time, and last-minute alterations can render a rule nonapplicable. If the rule says, for example, "Don't go out into the street," what is a child to do if his baby sister wanders out into the street? Should the big brother just stand there and not rescue his baby sister?

Monitor both observance of the rule by your child as well as the rule's relevance and usefulness. Be willing to entertain a violation of the rule under appropriate extenuating circumstances. When you find a violation of a valid, applicable rule, confront the child about it. If you think a disciplinary conse-

quence is merited, follow the procedures for logical consequences given later in this chapter.

Indicate your specific expectations. It's best to tell your
child what you want him to do and not to do. If your child is
to fix a snack unsupervised, list
acceptable snack items. Don't
leave a note that says something
like "Don't eat any junk food."

Always indicate the specific
desired behavior. Instead of
"Please clean your room," have a
photograph of the properly
arranged and cleaned room on
the wall as a visual guide and
leave a note such as "Please empty
the wastebasket and dust under
the bed." Be sure to include exact
actions you want your child to take. Instead of "Be nice to your
sister," say "Please show her how to dress her doll."

> Just because a rule was broken doesn't mean that the child must face a disciplinary consequence.

Give Anger-Control Training

ABUSE OF ANGER is among the many tricks of the trade for
oppositional children and teens. Because anger is primarily a
protective mechanism, it has important functions to aid psychological adjustment. Your child needs to learn how to use it
wisely. I detailed the definition of anger in chapter 2.

The best handling of anger involves putting its effects to
good use in three different ways. The two most prominent
physiological effects are a narrowing of mental focus and an increase in energy. When angry, your child becomes bullheaded
and squirmy. The three different ways to train your child to use
anger are summarized by the acronym ACE. Teach your child
to play the ACE of anger:

A—Use anger to adapt. Train your child to use the burst of energy and the increased determination given by the anger to change his approach to the situation. If he is becoming frustrated about his grades, for example, he can use that extra energy to study harder. His increased mental focus will automatically aim his concentration at the target behavior that needs to be adapted. He needs to listen to what his anger is telling him and follow its lead. If he is becoming angry at the fact that his shoes keep slipping off, maybe it's time for a new pair.

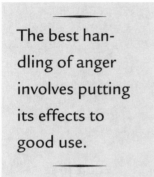

The best handling of anger involves putting its effects to good use.

C—Use anger to confront. By enacting the A of the ACE of anger, your child stops hurting himself. By enacting the C, he gets others to stop hurting him. He uses the burst of energy and the determination to tell whoever is bothering him about his needs and request a change for the better.

I have developed a simple three-part sequence to assist any child in confronting others who are being bothersome. This method is ideal to use when siblings, classmates, or playmates are doing things that could lead to potential conflict. Let's say, for example, that your son is bothered when his sister wants him to talk with her and play table games with her when he is doing his homework:

• **Part 1: Please stop . . .** The first part involves telling the other person distinctly to discontinue the irksome behavior that is creating the difficulty. The correct phrase begins with the two words "Please stop," then your child describes the observable disturbing behavior. In our example, he would say, "Please stop talking to me when I'm trying to do my homework." Notice the first word in his sentence and make sure he notices it, too!

- **Part 2: Please do . . . instead.** The second part involves describing exactly what the other person can do instead in order to resolve the situation. This feature elevates this procedure above merely telling somebody off because it holds your child responsible for coming up with a solution. In our example, he would say, "Please go into the dining room, set up the game, and wait for me there, rather than talking to me now." Again, notice the first word in his sentence and make sure he notices it, too!

- **Part 3: I'll do . . . for you.** The third part involves describing what the offended person will do in support of the changes asked for in the second part. The main message is "If you'll do that, I'll do this for you."

  Notice that the emphasis is on the needs of the other person. Keeping such a focus helps build conscience. In our example, he would say, "If you do that, I'll come into the dining room in a few minutes and play with you, after I'm done with my homework."

E—Use anger to escape. In most circumstances, encourage your child to play the A and the C, with heavier emphasis on the former. It will generally be easier for your child to change himself and his own behavior than to get others to change theirs. When neither the A nor the C solves the problem, there is one more option. I like to keep it in reserve, and I encourage children and teens to use the ACE in alphabetical order.

The third option is playing the E by removing himself from a situation in which his needs are under threat. Let's use the example that your son plays on a soccer team but resents going to practice and acts quite intolerable after each game. Finally, you begin to understand why. The coach belittles him, tells him that he can't dribble the ball as well as his teammates, keeps him on the bench through most of every game, and tells him to watch how his teammates play. No wonder he doesn't enjoy soccer practice or games! It's time to pull him out of soccer and put him into a more suitable activity, perhaps one that is not so competitive.

In the first two parts, the child is sticking up for himself. In the third, he is thinking of the other person's needs as well.

This simple three-part procedure is usable by just about any verbally fluent child or teen in just about any circumstance. It is an enactment of the age-old principle of harmonious relating: Love your neighbor (part three) as yourself (parts one and two).

Playing the ace is a tremendously useful strategy for handling anger. But there are additional anger-management tools you can use as a supplement to ACE.

Have a concerns notebook. A very effective way to handle anger is having a concerns notebook. Your child writes down whatever is bothering him in a special notebook that only he may write in. On a regular basis, he takes his notebook to an adult he trusts and discusses each item. He receives advice about how to play his ACE for each item in the notebook. The adult does not have to be a trained counselor and could be you or a sibling. The interviews can be as frequent as seems helpful. I have found once per week to be satisfactory for most of the children for whom I've incorporated this excellent technique in my clinical family practice.

Dump it off. Vigorous movement that involves symbolic discharge of anger is also generally helpful. Invite your child to run around the outside of your home, jump on a rebounder or athletic mat, jump on two mattresses set aside in a corner for that purpose, or use a jump rope. Punching bags are also an option; I recommend the large duffel size version, not the football size.

Talk It Out. After anger is discharged, it is important to sit down with your child and have an empathic heart-to-heart talk about the underlying emotional pain triggering the anger. Remember from chapter 2 that anger is always a secondary response to a primary hurt. You need to find the primary hurt, and the best time is immediately after some sort of vigorous anger-dumping exercise.

Try to suggest some ways in which your child can play the ACE of anger as well as resolve the underlying issues. Use the principles I outlined in chapters 4 and 5 as you have your anger-resolving conversation subsequent to anger-dumping exercise.

Anger moments are always valuable, because they give you excellent insight into the major sources of psychological pain in your child's life. They are like a road map for what you need to address to make life work better for your child. Remember that anger is always a *secondary* response to a *primary* hurt and that relieving the primary hurt is the most effective response to your child's anger.

Watch for Anger Abuses

WATCH OUT FOR two anger abuses commonly shown by oppositional children: dumping anger onto external objects and animals and having rage-type tantrums. Ideally, the anger should be "aimed" in an appropriate, related direction by playing the ACE—either at oneself or at the offending circumstance or persons. It should not involve kicking walls, slamming doors, being cruel to animals, or bullying weak target persons such as small children. Nor should its intensity be exaggerated to the rage level.

Something is drastically wrong if either of these two processes is occurring. If these types of anger issues keep resurfacing, get professional help for your child's anger management.

Movement therapies, such as art, music, and dance therapy, are often very useful. Sit-and-talk counseling is not as helpful for children under the age of eight as having a counselor work through you to assist your young child.

Realize Your Human Limitations

IF YOUR CHILD or teen is already deeply in trouble over an incident of profound misbehavior, no action of yours can redeem the event. The best thing you can do is to stand by as a helpful ally and allow the natural consequences to unfold. Sometimes, the answer to "Now what should I do to prevent any bad things from happening?" is "Nothing."

At such a time, consider your child to be symbolized by a cake that calls for 30 minutes of baking time and has already been in the oven for 20 minutes. It is too late to alter the cake's ingredients. Concentrate on controlling yourself. Avoid the trap of being perfectionistic or unrealistic about how much influence you can have. It may be that no action of yours can "make it all better."

Rely on Natural and Logical Consequences

NATURAL AND LOGICAL consequences are the best types of after-the-fact discipline to use with oppositional and defiant children and teens. They do a better job of keeping parents out of power struggles and of helping develop conscience than any other system of discipline. Of course, the ideal approach to misbehavior is to prevent it in the first place.

The punitive "gotcha" mentality that exists in many families is fraught with dangers and risks. I don't recommend punishment as a mainstay for child rearing. Humane consequences will do fine, thank you. There is no need to deliver exaggerated arbitrary pain to your children.

Logical and natural consequences are especially helpful because they provide the needed firmness to teach children the direct, specific, domino effects of their behavior. You can then stand by as a helpful ally without adding insult to your child's already fragile self-esteem.

Natural and logical consequences also teach important lessons when there is no misbehavior involved. Positive consequences provide motivation and form the building blocks of conscience.

> The ideal approach to misbehavior is to prevent it in the first place.

The natural consequence of saving a few dollars each month is having an easy and fun experience at Christmas shopping that year. The logical consequence of doing a favor for Mom is that Mom will be more willing to consent to a privilege that the child desires.

Take advantage of natural consequences. You don't apply natural consequences. You simply take advantage of them. My definition of natural consequences involves only four words: Whatever will happen anyway. Natural consequences are not manufactured by parents; instead, they are simply allowed to occur. The natural consequence of your child's grabbing a small dog's fur is being nipped by the dog; of running on an icy sidewalk, a skinned knee; of experimental puffing on a cigar, coughing and choking; of grabbing a playmate's toys, being rejected by that playmate. Natural consequences are spontaneous ways of learning about life and can be powerful teachers.

It would be irresponsible, even criminal, of course, to allow *every* natural consequence to occur without intervention. You don't allow a 2-year-old to pull a pan of boiling water down on his head to "teach him a lesson." But by the same token, unnatural intervention to shield from natural consequences children who *do* "know better" is an act of malparenting. If your teenager shoplifts, don't cover up the act and lie to the police on his behalf.

When you want a natural consequence to become a corrective influence on your child, don't intervene. Temporarily divorce yourself from the situation and be patient and quiet. Be your child's ally and avoid giving I-told-you-so speeches afterward.

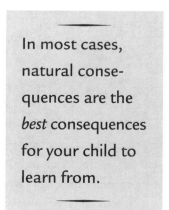

In most cases, natural consequences are the *best* consequences for your child to learn from.

If he brings up the event for discussion, express hope that he will change his actions in some way next time so that things work out more pleasantly for all concerned. Treat the experience as you would any mistake made by your child—an opportunity to learn and improve.

In most cases, natural consequences are the *best* consequences for your child to learn from. But what do you do when a natural consequence is inappropriate? When it might take too long to materialize or might jeopardize the child's health or safety?

Generate Logical Consequences

WHEN IT SEEMS inappropriate to permit a natural consequence, you can intervene in a humane, sensitive, and loving way. The consequence of the misbehavior can be your emotionally honest response to it, thus logically related to it. Logical consequences are known ahead of time by all concerned. You guide them, and your child experiences them as logical in nature.

If the conflict involves your child's tracking mud into the house, your emotionally honest response would be not to allow any more tracked-in mud. Inform him that he is to leave muddy shoes on a mat from now on and that he will have to mop up the kitchen if mud is tracked in. Notice the compensatory nature of the logical consequence—cleaning up the mess he made.

Logical consequences build conscience in children who misbehave. You actually use instances of misbehavior as teaching moments to rebuild in your child a proper sense of personal responsibility for the impact of his actions on other people and their feelings.

Explain ahead of time. Explain to your child the new actions you will take whenever the misbehavior occurs. Tell your child what you will do and let him decide what he will do. After your initial explanation, there is no need for nagging about your new policies. Simply take whatever action would be an emotionally honest response to enforce your intention.

> Logical consequences build conscience in children who misbehave.

Don't promise a specific action. Stay vague in describing what actions you'll take and avoid committing yourself to a specific consequential action. Manipulative children like to decide whether it is "worth it" to go ahead and disobey. If your child asks what you're going to do if he violates the rule, state that you will do whatever you need to do in order to demonstrate your intent and firmness on the matter.

Control yourself, not the child. When you set out to control an oppositional child completely, you are issuing an open invitation for a power struggle. When your child starts to misbehave, put the emphasis on controlling yourself rather than on controlling him. Stop cooperating with him. Don't do him any favors relevant to the misbehavior. Control what you will give to, do for, or permit for your child.

The concept of getting the emphasis off controlling the child confuses some parents, especially when they are used to the punishment mentality of discipline. There is, however, only one person in the world whom you can control. Be realistic and attempt to control only that person, not your child. You'll avoid many power struggles if you follow this guideline.

> Don't nag or scold. Let the consequence of misbehavior do the teaching.

Work before play. Set a time limit for your child's combined work and play. The longer he takes to do the dishes, the less time there will be for you to read a story because both must be accomplished by bedtime. Work must come before play. "As soon as you show me your homework, you may play your computer games." Teach your child my couplet: Work before play makes a happy day; play before work makes you a jerk.

Temporarily withdraw abused privileges. When your child violates or abuses a privilege you've extended, withdraw it and give him a chance to regain it later when he shows he can handle it responsibly. For example, temporarily deny him the use of his bicycle if he rides it carelessly or forbid him use of the computer temporarily if he hasn't used it properly. Don't accompany the experience with nagging and scolding. Let the consequence do the teaching.

Apply them calmly. Provide logical consequences firmly, dramatically, quickly, and calmly. The consequences should be fair, humane, and justified, not delivered with vengeance. Because they are so justified and humane, you should have no qualms about enforcing them.

No second chances. It is important not to allow an oppositional child an opportunity to manipulate his way out of facing the consequence. "Next time, you'll have another chance" is sufficient in response to any plea he may make for dodging a consequence. Most oppositional children try to debate consequences with their parents. Refuse to talk further on the matter.

Empathize with the distress. Although logical consequences will not make you the helpful ally that you could be when you allow natural consequences, you will at least not be the adversary that you become when authoritarian punishments are used. Your proper attitude should be one of mild regret that he has chosen to act in a way that has led to these consequences. Unlike punishment, your role is more of an empathic ally.

No nagging. Logical consequences are a form of natural consequences in that they reflect your honest emotional response to argumentative, pushy, oppositional children. Never refer to logical consequences with I-told-you-this-would-happen speeches. Try to replace nagging with one directive message; then combine the message with an enforcing action. Actions are the salad, and words the dressing, of effective parenting.

No blank checks. Oppositional and power-oriented children like to push for all they can get. Always put a condition on the privileges you extend. When responding to a request, try to use "yes, with conditions" rather than "yes, with a blank check." For example, say: "Yes, you may go over to Derek's house, as long as you call and ask his mother's permission and are home by 8:00."

Hold out hope. Because oppositional children want to argue and debate when they receive a "no," tack on the possibility of a "yes, later." For example, say: "No, you may not go over to Derek's house tonight, but we will see about inviting Derek over this weekend."

You automatically eliminate the usefulness of your child's debating skills by holding out a more attractive possibility.

Never promise anything. Defiant children like to trick parents into committing to something, then badger the parents into submission if they don't deliver what was promised. Stay out of that trap. The only thing you should ever promise is "We'll see how it goes." And "how it goes" means how you feel, based on how your child has acted in the meantime.

Use compensatory and payback logical consequences. I like compensatory types of logical consequences as discipline options for many reasons. In fact, I commonly teach in my seminars on ODD and ADHD that these types of arrangements are the closest parents should ever get to punishment.

The basic principle is that the child owes all offended or affected persons a fair payback for the inconvenience or distress caused by his misbehavior. Once he has made restitution, the issue is closed, and there are no additional penalties tacked on. The child learns many lessons about social responsibility, the impact of misbehavior on others, the importance of politeness and apology, and conscience. This approach allows the child to have a meaningful part in setting things right after a judgment error. And he does it all without experiencing any downgrading of self-esteem.

Time repayment. When argumentative stalling tactics or other misbehaviors cause you to waste time, your child owes you that amount of time in the form of helpful labor. If you had to take 10 minutes out of your day to deal with misbehavior, you receive 10 minutes of added help with chores that day.

Item replacement. If a child damages or breaks an item, he owes a replacement or repair to the owner of the item. If he doesn't have enough money to buy a replacement item, he earns the money from you and uses it to replace the damaged item. The final judge of whether the replacement was adequate is the offended person, not the child who committed the offense.

Apology. Apology is a verbal form of item replacement. The child repairs damage done to the feelings of the other person. A relationship-healing apology consists of eight steps. All eight just happen to begin with the letter A. They include doing a meaningful favor for the offended person.

A begrudging, mumbled "I'm sorry" is not sufficient nor is the false "conditional" apology: "If I lost your toy, I'm sorry." Worst of all is the blame-the-victim/blame-the-universe apology: "I'm sorry you got your feelings hurt" or "I'm sorry your toy got lost."

Rehearse honest apologies with your child and consider collapsing some of the points if giving all eight steps is too cumbersome.

Help Your Child Achieve Desired Goals

OPPOSITIONAL CHILDREN AND teens tend to be arrogant. Among the many ways they display that trait is their frequent tendency to want to have their cake and eat it too. Despite their misbehavior and contrary actions, they expect lost privileges to be given back, trust to be restored, and freedoms to be bestowed upon them.

They need to learn socially appropriate ways for building up life's little blessings. They can't be successful by simply demanding those kinds of services from others.

Earning back broken trust. If your child has lost your trust, it is his responsibility to earn it back, not yours to replace

The Eight A's of Apology:
How to Do It Right

Here are the eight aspects of a genuine apology. Role-play with your child to make sure he understands how to provide all of them when delivering an apology:

1. **Admit.** Admit you did the offending act.

2. **Account.** Explain what you were trying to accomplish or what you were thinking at the time.

3. **Acknowledge the wrong.** Indicate you are aware of the pain, hurt, or inconvenience you caused.

4. **Apologize.** Say you are sorry that you caused this offense and hurt.

5. **Ask forgiveness.** Say that you hope the person will forgive you.

6. **Affirm the relationship.** Indicate your desire to maintain or improve your relationship with the person.

7. **Amend.** Do a favor, bring a gift, do chores for the person, or invite the person to do something fun with you.

8. **Adjust.** Think about what you can do differently next time so that you won't repeat the mistake. Change something to prevent it from happening again.

it. The logical consequence of your child's lying about having accomplished the assigned chores is that you will supervise more closely next time. Your child needs to learn that people don't owe him renewed trust without some evidence on his part of its merit.

Earning back lost privileges. The way to gain a privilege back is to handle it more responsibly next time. The logical consequence, however, is a reduced privilege for next time. Your child might have to start back near ground zero to earn his way back up to the level of privileges he had before abusing the privilege. The logical consequence for staying out 30 minutes beyond the agreed upon time is having to come in 30 minutes earlier next time. When the child handles that new rule responsibly, another trial at the regular curfew is warranted.

> If your child has lost your trust, it is his responsibility to earn it back, not yours to replace it.

Earning increased freedom. Oppositional children and teens have insatiable appetites for freedom. When they receive some, they generally want more—pronto. The logical consequence for violating the privilege of freedom is more restriction and closer supervision next time. After next time occurs without incident, the amount of freedom can be increased. At any time, the child can earn more simply by honoring it and handling it responsibly.

With some extremely defiant and severely disruptive children and teens, you may need to stop relying on logical consequences altogether. Logical consequences work very well when used sparingly but not when piled onto each other excessively. Suppose, for example, that because of repeated, identical acts of defiance, you have removed *all* of your child's freedom. ("You're grounded from the computer, television, and every electrical appliance in this house for 38—no, make that 39—years.") You must avoid this type of downward spiral. Sidestep invitations to power struggle and avoid relying heavily on logical consequences if your child's pattern is one of chronic, entrenched, and frequently repeated power-oriented misbehavior. In such a case, the answer no longer lies in discipline techniques but in more basic issues having to do with your child's sense of being loved and emotionally safe. Seek professional counseling and put heavy emphasis on strengthening your child's or teen's sense of belonging and lovability within your family. Ask the counselor to read chapter 3 and to use it as a guide in assisting your family.

Teach Cooperation by Chores and Routines

CONTRIBUTING TO THE family order is an important and meaningful part of a child's learning to become a responsible person. A well-developed sense of personal responsibility goes a long way toward preventing oppositional misbehavior and attempts at power plays within the family. Household chores provide opportunities for learning self-discipline, promptness, neatness, reliability, and the importance of being helpful.

Unfortunately, daily chores and routines often become a seedbed for power conflicts between oppositional children and their parents. Almost any aspect can add fuel to the fire of contention—which chores, done by whose standards, by what time, at what time of day, under what conditions?

Have a regular chore time. If household chores are natural and expected parts of the daily routine, conflicts diminish. A regular family chore time works the best. The set time can be daily, weekly, or both. Try a brief tidy-up period before bedtime each day and on Saturday morning.

Get everyone involved. Give instructions for each chore. An oppositional child will have fewer complaints if you occasionally do some chores along with him. Develop a system to distribute chores among family members, a method of supervision and inspection, and the motivation or incentives you want to use. The goal of these arrangements is to get all family members, including oppositional children, involved in keeping everything clean, usable, and in its place.

Emphasize whole-family benefits. Don't let your child get by with "I didn't make the mess, so I shouldn't have to clean it up."

> Household chores provide opportunities for learning self-discipline, reliability, and the importance of being helpful.

Explain how chores help the family and why they are a shared part of family living. You might say, for example: "This home is our home, this family is our family, and these dishes are our dishes. The person doing dishes didn't eat off all the dinnerware, use all of the utensils, or drink from all the cups."

One meal served with dirty dishes as a logical consequence will convince even the most oppositional child of the foolishness of dodging the responsibility of contributing to clean dinnerware.

Don't overdo supervision. Stay as outwardly uninvolved as possible; avoid nagging and reminding. Supervise from a distance and randomly check on performance unless more stringent monitoring is needed. If you use too much pressure, an oppositional, contrary child will not feel a personal sense of ownership of the chore or pride in the accomplishment. The issue might then become a power struggle over your right to assign the chore. Repeated balking and grumbling about chores can often be remedied by breaking them down into smaller units.

Express genuine thanks. Clear, sincere appreciation for chores completed will help everything go smoother and minimize opposition from a defiant child. Comment on the large amount of effort shown. Nobody likes to try hard only to have others dismiss the effort by not seeming to notice or value it.

Keep chores small. Long, complicated chores mean trouble. They are harder to supervise, symbolize drudgery to the child, and are the first things complained about in family council meetings. Break them down into smaller units and assign the small chunks as individual chores.

Use charts. The more parents can stay out of verbal exchanges, the fewer power struggles an oppositional child will try to start. Follow the previous charting guidelines in this chapter.

Give choices. If you don't deal an oppositional child or teen some power cards, he will misbehave and invite power struggles in order to feel power. Always take advantage of choice-making opportunities to fulfill a resistant need for power. Arrange for each child to choose from among a few chore assignments each day. In chapter 7, I explain how to magnify your child's choice-making experiences. Such magnification is an important part of preventing power-oriented misbehavior, and chores are a convenient way to accomplish it.

Vary the chore menu. Oppositional children are quick to complain if a chore is unpleasant or boring. Rotate the array of chores every few weeks, so no child is stuck for long with a particularly unpleasant chore assignment. I recommend that children not be given repulsive chores such as toilet cleaning or trash handling when such an assignment is likely to be interpreted as an insult to their self-esteem.

Avoid interlocking chores. To prevent hassles from oppositional children, assign each child chores that are internally consistent and in separate locations from the chores done by other children. Put the chores on separate channels. Avoid interlocking chore assignments. Duane should not have to wait until Beth is done before he can start his chore. Each child should be able to complete the assigned chores whether or not the other children have done theirs.

Prevent untidy bedrooms. Many power-oriented children and teens like to display their defiance by decorating their rooms in an "early tornado" theme. Closing the door so others do not have to experience the room by sight, sound, or smell is probably the simplest solution, though it doesn't teach much in the way of self-care or conscience.

To encourage a clean, tidy bedroom, use structure to advantage by devising a place for everything. Color code and label dresser drawers. Place hooks on the wall. Use dishpans as bins and provide numerous shelves, bins, and small, sturdy cardboard storage boxes. Color code the bins and boxes for different purposes—building blocks in the red bin, paper and pencils in the white bin, doll clothes in the pink box, for example.

> Many power-oriented children display defiance by decorating their rooms in an "early tornado" theme.

Another useful approach is to offer to help your child or teen clean up the room and, at the same time, provide increased structure to prevent future deterioration to the pigsty level. For the very defiant teen, I suggest the therapeutic affection

confrontation method described in chapter 5, conducted in the front seat of your car while the teen is consuming a favorite food from a restaurant. Point out that the disorganized, messy bedroom does more harm than good and offer to help decrease its overall chaos while still allowing your teen the "privilege" of living in a relatively messy environment.

Have a minimum of furniture. The fewer items of furniture, the more easily your child will locate toys and other items within the room. If only one child is using the room, a bunk bed provides an excellent storage area that quickly transforms into a bed for overnight guests. A hamper (covered and decorated by the child), a wastebasket, and adequate shelving are essential structural aids. Consider converting half the closet into shelves.

Avoid Unrealistic Consistency

SUPPOSE YOU PROMISE a trip to a favorite store in the evening, but your child misbehaves during the day. Which

type of consistency do you show? Do you show consistency by
following through on your promise or show the consistency of
reflecting your true feelings by going back on your promise?
Avoid these misguided attempts at consistency:

Evenness of mood. "I will always smile and be pleasant to
all of my children (even though my sleep, nutrition, and
stresses vary greatly and the children's behavior fluctuates)."

Values and standards identical. "What is unacceptable behavior in one child is also unacceptable in any other: If it is
wrong for Dana to do it, then it is wrong for Brian to do it
(even though Brian and Dana handle responsibilities entirely
differently)."

Follow-through and determination. "Because I promised
that I would do this favor for Deena, I'll do it (even though I
don't feel like it anymore because of the way she acted after I
made the promise)."

Universality of rules. "The same rules and consequences
apply for all of the children. Since I won't let Andy climb on it,
I won't let Suzanne climb on it either (even though Suzanne
uses great care and won't hurt herself)."

Maintaining airtight routine. "We don't do what Cyndi is
asking for. We've never done it before so she can't do it (even
though this circumstance is a unique opportunity for Cyndi)."

Pairing actions to consequences. "Every time Sondra does
that, this will happen to her as a consequence (even though the
circumstances and her intentions are different from time to
time)."

Equivalence. "What I do for one child, I will do for all
(even though some may not want it done and others are des-
perately seeking it)."

Parental agreement. "We must always agree on every aspect of raising our children (even though we differ in dozens of
other ways and sometimes don't have the same perspective on a
situation)."

Use Wisdom in Consistency

IN CONTRAST TO these misguided forms, two types of consistency actually work. Manage consistency with congruent and contemporaneous treatment of your child. Your child receives useful feedback about the impact of his behavior on others, which is the cornerstone for the development of conscience.

Congruence. Match feelings and actions. Act according to how you feel, giving a direct and honest indication of your reaction to your child's behavior or to your own circumstance. While congruence is one of the most important forms of consistency to maintain, it can conceivably be abused. When I encourage you to be congruent, I'm not advocating that you start being unreliable, dishonest, manipulative, abusive, or unkind or that you needn't hold to your word if you simply don't feel like it. When you have an *important* need that gets in the way of following through, stay true to your feelings: "This is how I feel, so this is what I am going to do. I feel this way in part because you acted the way you did." "I know I promised to take you shopping, but I'm just too tired right now. I'll rest a bit and try to arrange to take you later today or tomorrow. I'm sorry."

> The safest, most reliable consistency is to provide whatever each child needs and is ready for.

Contemporaneous treatment. Treat a child according to his individual readiness. Provide guidance needed by a specific child at the moment, regardless of whether a similar action would have been taken with a different child: "I'll let you go over to Sam's house because you have been so helpful to me with Tammie, even though we don't usually let anyone from our family visit Sam at this time of day." Discourage demands by siblings for equal privileges. Substitute instead the concept of equally special privileges that are uniquely suited to each child. The safest, most reliable consistency is to provide whatever each child needs and is ready for.

Arrange for Night-Out Privileges

AMONG THE MOST common of contentions between parents and teens are those surrounding trips out into the community at night and during nonschool days. How can you be assured that all is well without seeming to be overcontrolling to your teen?

Make a deal. You agree to be as accommodating as possible to your teen's wishes with regard to going out in the evening. In exchange, your teen provides five items of information for you. These items are the minimum needed for you to be assured that all is well. Your permission for this excursion pivots on both your knowledge and your approval of:

• **Who:** With whom will your teen be spending the evening?

• **What:** What will your teen be doing?

• **When:** When is your teen leaving home and planning to return?

• **Where:** Where is your teen going?

• **How:** What assurances can your teen provide that he will be safe and that he won't be involved in any behaviors that put him at risk? How will he get home? How will he contact you if he gets sidetracked? How can you contact him?

This is the bare minimum of information your dependent child or teenager may provide. You are free to ask for additional information, of course, but be sure your teenager understands that the law itself requires you to know and approve of these

Five Fingers for Night-Out Privileges

Hold up your hand and refer to each of the five digits. Touch each as you state what you want from your teen before granting permission for that excursion: who, what, when, where, and how. The five things you want are the five aspects that every parent has a right to know. The fifth finger, representing safety, can be summarized as "Give me a phone call if anything changes or you have any problems."

factors. Your teen has no legitimate reason for withholding this information. For you to settle for less would be an act of child neglect and would put you at legal risk.

The key to reducing and eliminating oppositional and power-oriented misbehavior is to encourage the development of a strong conscience. The central focus of discipline for oppositional children and teens should be prevention of misbehavior. Create emotional safety, provide encouragement, establish need-meeting routines and structure, and free up emotional communication processes so the child can express needs calmly and verbally rather than by acts of misbehavior. If misbehavior occurs, the first step is confrontation, as discussed in chapter 5.

Only after all of these steps are taken should you have to resort to the various principles and techniques described in this chapter.

Redirecting your child's talents for assertion into constructive avenues provides a key for successful adjustment. The final chapter describes effective, life-changing things to do with all that creative energy and determination the oppositional child has.

7

Help Your Child Use Power Wisely

O NE OF YOUR child's major life tasks is to explore the best use of personal power. The oppositional child abuses power. A key to successful parenting of a defiant child is giving permission, guidance, and examples of how to be strong. Your child needs to experience strength in a socialized, win-win fashion that considers the needs of others.

Give Your Child Legitimate Personal Power

WHEN THEY'RE YOUNG and needy, children tend to push things as far as they can. They want their parents and the world to operate according to their own fancies and whims. As they mature, children find out what works and what doesn't in the lifelong task of getting personal needs met. As these lessons are being learned, children also increase their skills at getting along with others.

Power needs are normal. Children's experiencing of their own power is similar to the natural tendency of a gas to expand until it reaches a firm barrier or wall. A bucket of household cleaning ammonia, for example, will quickly fill a kitchen with a strong, sharp odor. The same bucket placed in a gymnasium will almost as quickly create the odor there. In a similar way, children push and expand to experience their power until the parent provides a "wall." This natural tendency to keep pushing occurs regardless of how far the parent has allowed the child to push before setting the limit. Problems develop when a parent sets limits that are too narrow or too wide.

Avoid stifling choice-making. Limits that are too narrow mean that the parents are showing off their own power and are not giving the children enough opportunities to learn to handle theirs. The bossy parent, the rigid and preachy parent, the critical parent, and the parent who makes too big an issue of mistakes and too small an issue of efforts and successes tend to force children to use detour methods of experiencing personal power.

Increase self-esteem. Children who don't have enough self-confidence see the world as a scary place and other people as bullies. They see themselves as weak, inadequate, vulnerable, at risk, not measuring up, and victims. These beliefs color all aspects of their movement through life. They tend not to be enthusiastic in the classroom. They are either too hesitant and underassertive on the one hand or too brash and misbehaving on the other. They tend to distort their memory of events in the past by thinking "if only" they had done this differently. They "Yes, but . . ." good news in the present and "Yes, but what if . . ." potential challenges in the future. They need to learn to assess the realities of life more accurately and then to accept those realities without these distortions.

Conversely, if a child experiences personal strength through safe and profitable assertion of needs, there is no need for detour methods. The way is open for meeting life's challenges head-on.

Hold Family Council Meetings

MANY CHILDREN BELIEVE they have little or no voice in family affairs. Family gatherings offer an excellent opportunity for children to participate in decision making and working things out together. Informal get-togethers are fine, but you can upgrade the entire process by regularly scheduled weekly family business meetings. This procedure is more commonly known as the family council.

The family council is one of the most powerful tools for rebuilding and maintaining a new level of harmony in your family. It allows your children a voice in family affairs while providing you with a useful avenue for exercising your leadership. It provides children excellent opportunities to exert influence in a socially appropriate way. They learn to stay tuned in to the needs of the entire family when sharing in decisions. Selfishness and bullheadedness diminish, as does oppositionality in general.

> The family council allows your children a voice in family affairs while providing you a way to exercise your leadership.

The family meets at an appointed time to discuss issues, make plans, voice concerns, solve problems, agree on solutions, and celebrate their love for one another. A typical family council meeting has a schedule that might look something like this:

Formal introduction. This meeting needs some way of distinguishing it from your everyday family activities and

discussions. It also needs a way of becoming a family-strengthening tradition. So your family council should begin and end the same way each week, with a formal, distinctive event that marks the beginning and ending. Depending on the ages, tolerance level, and habits of your family, you might sing a song, ring a bell, read an inspirational thought, pray together, distribute bowls of ice cream, or even tell an introductory joke.

Review of last week's activities. Discuss the pleasant activities during the preceding week to refresh memories and to bring everyone up-to-date. This time provides an excellent opportunity to share each other's joys and successes.

Notes from the previous meeting. Read aloud the notes from the preceding meeting. They include the issues discussed as well as the agreements, decisions, and plans that were made.

Personal schedules. Transportation, child care, meals, and similar routines may need to be modified during the upcoming week. All members know where everyone is going and, in general, what everyone is doing. This segment is when those all-important parent-child pairings can be arranged.

Family projects. The family discusses upcoming recreational activities as well as work projects. Decisions are made about how the family will spend the upcoming weekend. Holiday plans, including gifts and contacts with relatives, are discussed in this segment.

Chores and routines. Any family member can make suggestions for changing daily or weekly routines about clothing, meals, housework, lawn care, pet care, car care, room cleaning, and related issues. Chores can become cutthroat issues in families with an oppositional child, so this segment becomes very useful for restoring peace and harmony.

Concerns and negotiations. Discuss items dealing with long-range family plans, such as vacations, job changes, moving, holidays, or household remodeling. You can also discuss any difficulties or conflicts that any family member is experiencing. Another crucial segment to prevent oppositionality, the discussion of everyone's concerns, is a singular replacement for balking, arguing, and defiance. Make sure everyone has a chance to voice concerns and express opinions on important issues affecting family life.

Recording of agreements. One person takes on the secretarial duty of writing or tape recording the agreements and the plans made during the meeting.

Lesson. On a rotating basis, the various family members make use of visual aids or other entertaining elements to present a lesson involving religious, moral, or social values. Usually, the lesson consists of a presentation followed by discussion.

Allowances. Discuss financial matters and distribute allowances to the children. It's amazing what handing out money can do to the willingness of children and teens to attend a family meeting!

Celebration. The council meeting closes with games, singing, storytelling, refreshments, or some similar celebration of family life. With a little advance planning, the celebration can become a basis for regular parent-child togetherness for the purpose of preparing and cooking the refreshments.

Get the Most from Your Family Council

THOUGH IT PROVIDES many functions to upgrade the quality of your family life, the family council's most important function is probably going to be that of decreasing oppositionality among the children in your family. To guarantee this result, guard each child's right to express concerns and opinions, so your children sense their growing impact on the family's decisions.

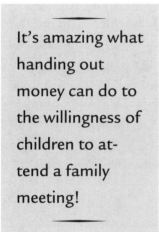

It's amazing what handing out money can do to the willingness of children to attend a family meeting!

There is nothing wrong with an oppositional child getting his own way—as long as others are not hurt or violated in the process. What is unacceptable are selfish, one-way decisions that amount to a win-lose situation. Staunchly defend win-win solutions as the only ones you are interested in. Those solutions come by awareness of each other's wants and needs, not through selfishness.

Emphasize Whole-Family Needs

ENCOURAGE A SPIRIT of inquiry: What is the situation? How does it look to each family member? What would be best for the *whole family?* Maintain respect for everyone's viewpoint and everyone's right to make choices. As the children learn that their opinions are valued, they will put more thought into them.

Don't let your family council deteriorate into a gripe session. Each person expressing a complaint should present one or more suggested solutions. The emphasis is on what the family, as a whole, can do to prevent a certain difficulty from arising in the future.

Seek win-win solutions. The decisions in the family council are made by consensus, with each family member participating. Agreement occurs only when all family members, not just the majority, can go along with the proposed plan of action. If no agreement occurs, postpone decisions until the next family council or use an experimental decision temporarily.

Consensus differs from majority rule, in which those who disagree are outvoted. Notice that agreements are win-win solutions. Majority rule, on the other hand, is like competition; it is a win-lose arrangement. For an oppositional child, always point toward win-win and away from competition and other win-lose arrangements.

Make the first meetings fun. The first few family council meetings should be oriented toward making plans for pleasant activities, such as deciding about weekend projects or vacations. In this way, the family can become accustomed to the concept of regular meetings without having to face difficult or touchy negotiations.

Everyone gets a chance. One way to help ensure a high level of openness of communication is to rotate the positions of chairperson, refreshment preparer, lesson giver, and secretary. Provide a notebook or bulletin board on which family members can write the concerns and issues they wish to discuss.

All members are invited to participate, but attendance should be voluntary. The best way to lure an uncooperative

Family Meeting Fun

Kristine and Scott are the parents of a large blended family. They decided during their engagement that no matter how busy family members got, their weekly family meeting would take precedence. The family meeting would be mandatory. In the beginning, the older kids were resentful, and the younger kids were badly behaved. Then Kristine and Scott decided family meeting didn't have to be productive; it only had to be fun. So they stopped taking it quite so seriously. The kids expressed a desire to play games, so Kristine and Scott made a trip to a large toy retailer and purchased about a dozen classic board games, card games, and other activities that required the entire family to interact. The kids now race home from school to bake cookies or other treats for weekly family meetings. Family business often consists of silly comments—"I want a pet unicorn." "I can almost bite my own elbow." "I'm the prettiest person in the room."

Kristine and Scott say family meetings have been the most important thing they've done to create unity in a diverse family, and they intend never to stop.

family member into participation is to conduct effective and interesting meetings. Eventually, the member will participate, out of curiosity if for no other reason. Even preschoolers can participate to some degree in family council meetings. Certainly, the younger children can help prepare or serve the refreshments. With the aid of a tape recorder, even a nonreader can serve as secretary for the meeting.

Decrease Sibling Rivalry

SIBLING RIVALRY OFTEN accompanies oppositional misbehavior. Do everything possible to reduce contention between the children in your family. Always push away from competition in your family, in the child's classroom, and in extracurricular activities. A competitive environment breeds defiance and oppositional tendencies. Sibling rivalry and competition go hand in hand.

Emphasize individuality. To the extent that each child feels affirmed as a unique individual, there is less need to be treated the same as siblings. Each child has a separate bedroom or area of a bedroom, a separate circle of friends, unique treats on holidays, and so forth.

Encourage kindness. Support any of your children's actions and statements reflecting courtesy, negotiation, sensitivity, and cooperation. Comment on how good both children feel after such exchanges, and indicate the warm feeling you have inside when you witness such kindness occurring between the siblings.

> A competitive environment breeds defiance and oppositional tendencies.

Encourage sharing. Counter all egotism and selfishness about time, ideas, or material objects. Encourage the sharing of skills, knowledge, ideas, and things. We love those whom we serve and help.

Teach assertion skills. Train your children to discuss and settle issues by mutual consent after exploring each other's wants, rather than by bullying or competing. Encourage them to ask directly for what they want, rather than screaming, whining, hitting, or grabbing.

Always use positive wording. Instead of saying: "Don't whine for that," say: "The way to ask is 'May I please have that?'"

Defuse volatile situations. Your child might misbehave simply to gain attention from other children. Give any pestered child some simple ways to defuse the situation so intense conflict doesn't have a chance to develop. If one child starts being a nuisance, the other child has three alternatives: (1) leave the scene, (2) get the other child to stop being a nuisance, or (3) agree to pay attention to the bothersome child. Telling the annoyed child to ignore the antics of a bothersome child often doesn't solve anything and goads the misbehaving child to intensify attention seeking.

Being Weak Is Damaging

A DIFFERENT SET of problems develops if parents display too little of their own power and allow their children to experience too much power. The parent who worries about every whim of the child, who waits on the child, who overprotects, who does for the child what the child can and should do without help, and whose peace-at-any-price philosophy avoids all conflict puts the child in the position of dominator of the family. The child's natural tendency to experience as much power as the parent will allow then leads him to demand, bully, and dominate even more.

The more your child dominates you, the less respect he has for you. The awareness of these kinds of feelings is scary for any child and throws off the parent-child relationship in many ways. It is as if the child can't help pushing more against the parent but becomes more afraid at seeing the parent so weak in response to the pushing.

Being weak is no role for a parent. What would make the child feel better is the parent's being strong, yet calm, while resisting the pushing. Don't merely comply with a power-drunk child. Set a reasonable limit on how much you will sacrifice your own needs for the sake of pleasing your child. Assert yourself and don't allow a violation of your rights by the child. Your demonstration of personal power and strength in these ways gives the permission your child needs to adopt a similar style of showing personal strength. If you are also strong, your child's power can be legitimate and safe, and your child can exercise it without fear of the scary results that happen when the parents are too weak.

Encourage control of self. The general principle to teach your child is to show strength by self-control, not by controlling others. Your strength in guarding your own rights and seeing that your own needs get met sets the best example. If, at the same time, you avoid domination and criticism, you help set up a situation that gives your child permission to seek and experience legitimate personal power.

> Teach your child to show strength by self-control, not by controlling others.

Encourage healthy independence. It is a tragic mistake to be intimidated by the idea of your child becoming independent. Being independent doesn't mean being rebellious. Every child must eventually attain a heightened level of personal decision making and influence, to the point of no longer requiring protection and guidance from parents. To be independent is to be nondependent. Be glad to support timely movement toward independence in your child or teen. With your teen's experience of gradually increasing personal autonomy comes less need to power struggle with you in order to feel strength.

Hunt for ways to put more and more facets of daily living increasingly under your child's control while simultaneously decreasing your influence. Gear this entire process to the overall maturity level your child seems to be attaining as time goes on. **Help chores go smoothly.** Contributing to the family order is an important miniaturized version of being a breadwinner and functioning independently in the world. Through performing regular household chores, your child learns many valuable lessons. My preference is to keep allowances for the most part loosely tied to chore accomplishment, including an occasional bonanza chore of extra proportions. A "salary plus commission" plan seems to work well. Each child receives an automatic baseline salary of income just for being a family member and can earn additional funds by choosing from among chore options. The mechanics of setting up chore arrangements were discussed in detail in chapter 6.

Find Leadership Opportunities

OPPOSITIONAL CHILDREN ARE born leaders. They gravitate toward situations in which they can experience being influential. To the extent that you fill this need, your child is less likely to exercise it in the form of power struggles and misbehavior.

Ask other adults in your child's life whether there are leadership opportunities that could be used for this purpose. Perhaps your child could do a survey at school, write an article or take pictures for the community newspaper, or make announcements over the loudspeaker or at athletic events. **Find a rank-ordered hierarchy.** Consider getting your child involved in community organizations, clubs, or athletic groups that would provide leadership experience. Hunt for a position in which your child or teen has specific responsibilities and a defined domain of influence. Perhaps your teen would benefit by joining an organization such as civil air patrol, a mountain rescue unit, or ROTC. These kinds of organizations feature an assigned rank within a power hierarchy.

Consider mentoring. Mentoring involves your teen's providing a trusting, giving relationship with one or more younger teens or children in a supervised setting. Some schools have organized mentoring programs available for interested teens. Most require at least a six-month commitment. Your teen might also want to consider similar activities, such as helping with the youth athletic program in your community, being an assistant coach for a children's athletic team, tutoring, church youth group leadership, and service in character-building organizations for children and youth.

Help your child feel more respected. Inviting power struggles is sometimes a way of saying "be impressed by me." To decrease oppositionality, eliminate the need for your child to fight for recognition and status. Review the thorough discussions in chapters 3 and 4 on how to upgrade any child's sense of being noticed, cherished, and admired. Put heavy emphasis on fulfilling your child's sense of belonging.

Encourage choice making. Allow your oppositional child or teen to make choices in the areas that reflect personal taste. Your child's grooming, clothing styles, preference in music, use of toiletry items, cosmetics preferences, jewelry, and food tastes are all up for grabs. There is no need for you to dominate in those areas.

Giving your child considerable leeway with regard to these aspects of daily living can sometimes be very helpful in building a bond of trust and mutual respect. When allowed to express individuality through legitimate channels such as these, your child may find less need to demonstrate uniqueness by oppositionality and rebellious antics.

Filter the help you give. Never do for a child what the child could accomplish without outside help. If you do anything for your child that he could do independently, you rob your child of a feeling of personal strength. The next step is a power ploy by your child to regain a semblance of power. Filter the help you give so that your child feels like a credible contributor to all accomplishments.

> Never do for a child what he could accomplish without outside help—or you rob him of a feeling of personal strength.

Help during part of a task. Give help only during the beginning, only during the middle, or only during the end of a task your child is trying to accomplish.

At the beginning: "All beginnings are difficult . . . go ahead and start . . . I'll help you get started."

During the middle: "You get started, and I'll check back in a few minutes . . . I'll be back in a while to see how you're doing . . . call me after you've started."

At the end: "I'll finish it off for you . . . tell me when you're just about finished . . . I'll help you check it over after you're done."

Be available when asked. As a guarantee against overinvolvement in your child's achievement, let your help be available but withhold it until your child asks for it. Say, for example, "You know where to find me. Call me if you need me. I'm available to help if you want my help."

Give limited necessary help. Put a speed governor on the amount of help you give. Help only when necessary and turn as much of the project back over to your child as possible. Don't be unwilling to help but be ready to pull back at any time when you notice your child's ability to take over the project.

Give bite-sized help. Dole out your help in little pieces. Let's suppose, for example, that your child can't find the answer to an open-book test question. You might first remind him about using the index and glossary. When your child finds the relevant section of the chapter, suggest finding a heading that would seem to be relevant, then a paragraph that would be most likely to contain the answer. At each step, give only the minimum help necessary to take your child to the next logical step in approaching the task.

Aim Toward Mastery

THE INTRINSIC REWARD of accomplishing academic and other kinds of tasks for your child should be a feeling of mastery of the environment combined with sensing an increase in knowledge, skills, and competence. Too often, though, the apparent motive for study is "get the teacher off my back" or "get a good enough grade to pass" or "earn money from parents for grades I get." Such external and trivial motives won't build character, self-confidence, or diligence. Nor will they decrease oppositionality.

Make sure school is working. School is the obvious arena for developing a feeling of accomplishment. To get the maximum benefit, your child or teen must believe that school is need fulfilling. Work with teachers to have school become relevant, meaningful, and a path to what your child wants in life. Find the doors by which the school experience can truly reach and stretch your child. Encourage incorporating topics your child is intrinsically interested in or at least feels safe doing.

Enhance feelings of competence. One type of mastery besides controlling external objects is mastering skills. An oppositional child or teen is less likely to start power displays if the need for feeling powerful can be met by the buildup of considerable skill and talent. For this and other reasons, I advocate enrolling oppositional children in extracurricular and community-sponsored classes and hands-on apprenticeship programs. There is no need to be perfectionistic. Follow the guidelines in chapter 3 about encouragement. All you're hunting for is a growing feeling of personal competence. Feeling strong inside means less need to generate temporary feelings of power through oppositional misbehavior.

Consider forensics. My favorite career prediction for most oppositional children and teens is that someday they will make good lawyers. Until then, however, their parents experience the brunt of those fabulous argumentative talents. In many high schools, there is an arena that is almost ideal for oppositional teens. It is the speech department in general and the debate team in particular. High school debate teams literally practice proving how right they are in verbal sparring matches. Sound familiar?

> Feeling strong inside means less need to generate temporary feelings of power through oppositional misbehavior.

Consider body movement talents. Dance, martial arts, yoga, bodybuilding, jogging, swimming, hiking, roller-skating, juggling, aerobics, gymnastics, exercise to music, belly dancing, and similar programs not only are invigorating but relieve tension and build self-confidence.

Control the environment, not the people. A gigantic mistake made by oppositional children and teens is trying to control people in order to be happy. When their attempts amount to misbehavior and disruption of orderly processes, neither they nor others end up any happier. Their solution is a lose-lose event. Do what you can to get your oppositional child or teen to aim the desire to control away from people and onto animals and material objects. These types of activities tend to decrease oppositionality because they fulfill the need to control.

Make things better. Encourage hobbies that involve solving mechanical problems or removing physical obstacles, such as maintenance and repair of engines or computers. There is a certain adventure in figuring out what is going wrong and definitely a certain power in making it right again.

Volunteer. Don't overlook opportunities to have significant impact on people in a prosocial way that doesn't involve illegitimate displays of power. Experiences that have worked to decrease oppositionality in teens include serving as a candy striper in a hospital, helping in a soup kitchen, reading to a blind person, assisting at a homeless shelter, collecting for medical research, and participating in blood drives. Animal-related service would include assisting at a shelter, providing foster care for animals awaiting adoption, and providing pet care for vacationers.

Organize things. Another alternative is hobbies involving gathering, collecting, and organizing. There are hundreds of types of "collections," from butterflies to gum wrappers. The child feels a great sense of control—in fact, total domination—over what to collect, the size of the collection, how it is stored and displayed, and so forth.

Make things prettier. Beautifying and enhancing the world makes anybody feel good. Lawn care, some forms of art, and environmental cleanup activities are examples of ways to feel powerful while doing good. Don't rule out planting flowers along a roadway or in a park and trimming the lawn of an elderly neighbor.

Construct things. Art and construction crafts are excellent ways to feel both competent and powerful. Ceramics, painting, glass working, construction toy sets, sculpture, collage, woodworking, metalworking, and related activities give a great sense of accomplishment.

Control animals. Pet care in general and dog training in particular can fulfill the need to control. The child is in charge of a dependent living creature. If your child wants to be the boss, why not boss a compliant, loyal animal in an organized, legitimate way?

Compose things. Musical, literary, and theatrical productions provide opportunities to experience the power of creative self-expression. Consider enrolling your child in classes on poetry, creative writing, storytelling, puppetry, choreography, calligraphy, or short-story writing.

Gear Freedom and Privileges to Responsibility

BELIEVE IT OR not, too much freedom can be scary for an oppositional child or teen. Despite their apparent claims to the contrary, they don't want to experience truly excess freedom. They simply want enough freedom so that they can feel sufficient power to compensate for their feelings of weakness. Granting too much freedom might be interpreted as meaning that parents don't care about what happens to the child.

Conversely, too little freedom may put an extra burden on parents because they would probably have to check on the oppositional child more often. The child would probably resent the excess restrictions, interpreting them as an indication of a lack of parental trust. Another obvious problem is that the child would be deprived of some key opportunities to learn how to make life decisions based on sound independent judgment.

A parallel issue is that of responsibility. Too little or too much responsibility can be harmful to any young person. The most practical solution is to discuss both topics with your child during the personal private interview (PPI) described in chapter 3.

When your oppositional child demonstrates enough responsibility to handle a slight increase in freedom, grant it. If unable to handle the current level of freedom responsibly, reduce it.

A flexible, tolerant attitude by parents will help this negotiation process. Have faith in your child's ability to learn to handle gradually increasing freedoms responsibly. When your child makes mistakes in an unsupervised setting, withdraw that particular freedom or privilege temporarily. Return it when your child brings you a written game plan for how things will be different next time. This

> When your oppositional child demonstrates enough responsibility to handle a slight increase in freedom, grant it.

written plan can emerge from a PPI meeting, the result of input from both of you.

Often an oppositional child thinks he is ready for more freedom than parents believe he is. The solution is to grant only part of the desired freedom as an experimental or probationary test. If all goes well, increase the amount of freedom allowed. If not, use that fact as the starting point of discussing the changes your child needs to make in order to gain increased freedoms.

Set firm limits on freedom when issues such as health and safety, protection of the rights of others, and maintaining orderly routines within your family are at stake.

By following these suggestions, you can assume less of the burden of watching over, directing, and protecting your oppositional child. You can also have the joy of watching your child expand her horizons in many directions and gain an increased foothold in making life work.

A Final Word of Encouragement

THIS BOOK SUMMARIZES my accumulated experience of more than 30 years as a clinical family psychologist. Many of the ideas, principles, and specific techniques are of my own invention and deduction, and many come from various other sources.

I have provided you with hundreds of concepts and techniques for preventing or solving the types of problems you are most likely to confront as the parent, guardian, or other adult charged with supervision of a child with oppositional tendencies. My goal was to present you with a kaleidoscope of possibilities, a tool kit overflowing with practical, usable tools.

I don't want you to feel overwhelmed or intimidated because of the potential difficulties. Oppositional defiant disorder and its related conditions are serious business with serious consequences, not only for the child but also for the family and for society as a whole. However, most oppositional children are born leaders who can grow up to lead fulfilling lives and become well-adjusted members of society. The ultimate thing to do with their thirst for power is to redirect it toward constructive pursuits.

Please select and follow those suggestions you find most relevant to your particular circumstance. You shouldn't use a hammer when you need a screwdriver. There may be many suggestions in the pages of this book that aren't relevant for your child. Happily, you can ignore those suggestions and concentrate on the remaining ones that apply more directly for you.

Have confidence that improvement will come. Never let the negatives of oppositionality outweigh your awareness of the positive potentials for your child. Your gifts of time, resourcefulness, and commitment are priceless. They will help your child achieve the best possible adjustment and success. Both of you will emerge as real winners.

I await your feedback as to the helpfulness of the suggestions in this book. Numerous resources are available through A.D.D. Plus. Please feel free to visit www.ADD-Plus.com, write to A.D.D. Plus, P.O. Box 4326, Salem, OR 97302, or call 800-VIP-1-ADD (800-847-1233). You can also send e-mails to addplus@hotmail.com.

Boredom Prevention Ideas

THESE SUGGESTIONS WERE provided by many parents of hard-to-manage children who are successfully using a "fun idea list" to prevent boredom and misbehavior. These activities are effective in helping children channel their energy into constructive pursuits and can become the starting point for your own fun idea list. You will want to modify it and add to it to fit your family's specific needs.

Fun Idea List

Outdoor Play with Others

- Have a popcorn and fruit-drink stand.
- Camp in the backyard in sleeping bags or tents.
- Do water play with hose and plastic slide cloth.
- Have a water fight with squirt guns and cups, using buckets of water as the source of "ammunition."

Indoor Play with Others

- Make a tent with a sheet and a card table.
- Gather shoes from around the house and play shoe store.
- Using a comb, brush, cup with water, and towel, play barber or hairdresser.
- Put things in a mystery sack and give clues about what it is, allowing the child to reach into the sack and feel the object as the last clue.
- Make up a pretend radio or television interview and talk into a tape recorder.

Outdoor Solitary Play

- Watch the stars through a telescope.
- Look through binoculars.
- Work on gardening.
- Line up pop cans and throw pebbles at them.
- Draw pictures of your yard to show the seasons of the year.
- Make a collection of leaves from the yard.
- Volunteer to sweep a neighbor's sidewalk without pay.
- Train and groom pets.
- Build something for backyard (birdhouse, bird feeder).
- Earn money by washing cars or mowing lawns.
- Write or draw on the sidewalk with chalk.
- Collect interesting rocks.

Indoor Solitary Play

- Listen to music.
- Punch a punching bag.
- Make muffins.

- Make an item for a model railroad or toy car set out of popsicle sticks, toy logs, or building toys.
- Plan a day trip for the family.
- Write letters to relatives or friends.
- Make a crossword puzzle for family members to solve.
- Organize a home slide show.
- Make a collage out of pictures from old magazines.
- Practice a musical instrument.
- Start or work on a collection (stamps, butterflies, bottle caps, coins, trading cards).
- Make a "food bingo" card by cutting and pasting pictures of food from a magazine. Play bingo on the next trip to the supermarket.
- Make shadow pictures on the wall.
- Paste a picture on cardboard, then cut into pieces for a homemade jigsaw puzzle.
- Stand dominoes on end in a pattern or a long winding line, then knock them down.
- Write down some good charades titles and topics for the family to use later.
- Juggle with balloons.
- Use a tape recorder to record sounds around the home.
- Sort family photos and put them in an album.
- Make personalized stationery using stencils.
- Make holiday decorations such as ornaments.
- Measure things with a measuring tape then make up a quiz for family members about the measurement results.

Whole-Family Activities

- Have a backward dinner—dessert first.
- Tell a story-in-the-round in which each member adds the next passage to the story.

- Tell fill-in-the-blank stories in which each member adds a word when invited to do so by the storyteller.
- Watch home movies.
- Read aloud from a favorite book and act it out.
- Do a benevolent project anonymously for a needy person or family.
- Play musical instruments and sing.

Fun Idea Drawer

- **Arts and crafts.** Crayons, safe paints, pieces of sponge, paint brushes, art and drawing paper, colored construction paper, felt markers, colored pencils, watercolors, play modeling dough, stencils, glitter, white glue, cotton balls, rulers, sequins, buttons, yarn, hole punch, craft sticks, clothespins, oatmeal boxes, cardboard bathroom tissue rolls, stamp pad and stamps (make your own from foot pads), scissors, old magazines with pictures, used greeting cards, poster board.
- **Games.** Table game boards, markers, dice, and spinners; children's playing cards; carrom board (over 100 games and relatively indestructible).
- **Writing equipment.** Typing paper, notebooks and notebook paper, ballpoint pens, pencils, erasers, stationery for writing to friends.

Discussion and Study Questions

Y OU CAN USE this book for group study and discussion. Have participants read one chapter between each session and come prepared with answers to all the questions at each session. Numerous additional resources to assist with parent education classes and discussion programs are available from A.D.D. Plus, P.O. Box 4326, Salem, OR 97302; phone 800-VIP-1-ADD (800-847-1233); or www.ADD-Plus.com.

Chapter 1

1. Have those participants who are parents or grandparents of a hyperactive child describe at least two distinctive instances of oppositionality shown by that child.

2. Do a survey of prenatal factors represented by participants and share results.

3. Have one participant perform the exercise Discovering Everyone's Two Basic Needs with another group, then report results.

4. Have everyone write down their own C & D percent figures as well as their estimate of the figure for the other parent of the same child. Those who are willing can then share with the group.

5. Cite at least one specific incident you are aware of, in your own parenting or that of someone else, of each of the four patterns of overinvolvement described in this chapter: nagging, hypervigilance, overprotection, and overindulgence.

6. What surprised you the most about this chapter?

7. What were the three most meaningful sentences for you in this chapter?

Chapter 2

1. Cite a specific incident in which your child's not asserting honestly and openly for his or her wants was probably because of a feeling that it would not have been safe, and another similar incident because of a feeling that it would not have been profitable.

2. Give three examples of how your child overasserts his or her needs and wants.

3. Cite one example in which your child has sent each of the three messages of the oppositional child:
   • I will control me
   • I will control you
   • I won't let you control me

4. Pretend you are explaining Dr. Taylor's approach to someone who has not read this book. Give a one-paragraph ex-

planation of this sentence: "Competition is by its very nature a vertical process."

5. Cite one instance in which your child acted like each of the six roles of an oppositional child (sneak, competitor, etc.). Cite six instances altogether.

6. Why did Dr. Taylor say with regard to a power struggle: "If you're in it, you can't win it"?

7. Rate your child on the Taylor Hyperactivity Screening Checklist and share results with the group.

8. What surprised you the most about this chapter?

9. What were the three most meaningful sentences for you in this chapter?

Chapter 3

1. Pretend you are explaining Dr. Taylor's use of a wiener roast fork as an analogy to effective parenting.

2. Cite one instance in which you did, or did not, give your child what Dr. Taylor calls "the license to be real." What happened afterward?

3. Some people believe that the most important need teens have is to rebel. But Dr. Taylor says: "Actually their most important need is to define their personhood as a separate, unique entity from parents." Write a one-paragraph opinion statement on this issue and whether or not you agree with the author.

4. What are some forms of misbehavior that are likely to occur for a child who doesn't get enough of each of the legs of the Encouragement table? Provide several examples for each leg.

   Insufficient leg 1 misbehavior:
   Insufficient leg 2 misbehavior:

Insufficient leg 3 misbehavior:
Insufficient leg 4 misbehavior:

5. Have your child compose the list mentioned by Dr. Taylor of ten things he or she is good at and ten weaker areas. Or compose your best guess at what your child would include on such a list.

6. Comment on Dr. Taylor's recommendation: Reinforce choice-making power. Many people would say to decrease choices for an oppositional child. Why does Dr. Taylor recommend giving more choices to a child who is already being overly defiant and oppositional?

7. Cite one incident in which you did, or did not, follow Dr. Taylor's recommendation: Allow self-determined pacing. What happened as a result?

8. What surprised you the most about this chapter?

9. What were the three most meaningful sentences for you in this chapter?

Chapter 4

1. Your child has just insulted a friend in a fit of anger but now is saddened by the turn of events. Provide an empathy statement.

2. Why does Dr. Taylor recommend: "Try to keep corralling your child into congruence."?

3. Write a paragraph that summarizes what you could say that would reflect (1) how you feel, and (2) what you need in order to start feeling better for these instances: a) You have just had an upsetting phone call from a relative. Your child walks in and wants you to fix a snack for him or her. b) You worked hard to fix a special dinner. Your child insists that he or she didn't ask for it and shouldn't have to eat it.

4. Do a survey and cite several examples you notice by observing other parents in public places, shopping, etc. involving the undesirable roles from the table Encouraging Healthy Emotional Communication.

5. Suggest a structural solution for:
   - Dirty towels and clothes on bathroom floor
   - Clothes and paper on bedroom floor
   - "Mom, I can't find the homework I did last night"
   - "I can't do the dishes, because we don't have any soap."
   - Children fighting over which TV programs to have on

6. What surprised you the most about this chapter?

7. What were the three most meaningful sentences for you in this chapter?

Chapter 5

1. Cite a recent instance of your attempt to use ignoring as a discipline device. What happened afterward?

2. Dr. Taylor recommends choosing a special location for a major confrontation conversation. What do you think would be the ideal location if you were to confront your child about some major issues? Share with the group.

3. Write an "I have a dilemma" note that you might give to your child. If possible, have this note apply to an actual aspect of your child's behavior you would like to be different. Include the four parts:
   - Introduce the dilemma
   - State the fear
   - Defend against the fear
   - Proclaim your love motive

4. Suppose your child badgers and pesters you about wanting a higher allowance. Write down an example statement

for the right way, and another of the wrong way, to give the "what you are doing" part of the five-part universal confrontation message.

5. Use the entire five-part universal confrontation technique with someone and report results.

6. Use one or more of Dr. Taylor's recommended retorts to "I don't know" or "I don't care" smoke screens and report results.

7. Arrange a pit stop or huddle system, then try to find an opportunity to use it. Report results.

8. Your child was just caught lying about having accomplished several chores over the last few days that were actually not done at all. Write at least five messages you could give to your child that would be helpful and corrective without triggering defiance.

9. What surprised you the most about this chapter?

10. What were the three most meaningful sentences for you in this chapter?

Chapter 6

1. Make a chore chart using the three variables Dr. Taylor describes and bring it to the group for a Show-n-Tell of chore charts.

2. Using Appendix A, construct a Fun Idea List for your child and bring it to the group for a Show-n-Tell of Fun Idea Lists.

3. Most people would say that to solve problems of misbehavior, have more rules to govern behavior. But Dr. Taylor says "The fewer rules, the better." Explain Dr. Taylor's position, and your agreement or disagreement with that position.

4. Compose a note such as you might leave for your unattended child about these issues. Do it two ways; the right way and the wrong way according to Dr. Taylor's view on indicating your specific expectations:

   a) what your child should have for dinner that your child must prepare unsupervised
   b) how your child is to control TV watching by two younger children whom your child is watching for a few hours
   c) how your teen should handle the issue of gasoline when borrowing the family car for several hours.

5. Dr. Taylor says "The two most prominent physiological effects are a narrowing of mental focus and an energizing effect." Cite an example of each from your personal experience.

6. Teach Dr. Taylor's three-part confrontation message to your child and observe an instance of its use. Share with the group.

   Part 1: Please stop . . .
   Part 2: Please do . . . instead
   Part 3: I'll do . . .for you

7. Give your child a special notebook and instruct in how to use it as a Concerns Notebook. Have one conversation in which your child uses it. Share results with the group.

8. Somebody picks up your copy of this book and reads that a natural consequence means "whatever will happen anyway."
   That person then says that natural consequences sound useless. Defend them to that person. Write a one-or two-paragraph explanation of their advantages and benefits.

9. What surprised you the most about this chapter?

10. What were the three most meaningful sentences for you in this chapter?

Chapter 7

1. Explain Dr. Taylor's analogy that a child's quest for power is like an expanding gas.

2. Have a Family Fun Time for at least 20 minutes before the next session and report results.

3. According to Dr. Taylor, what is the most important function of the Family Council? Which aspects of the Family Council allow it to perform that function?

4. Of the many recommendations for decreasing sibling rivalry in this chapter, which three hold the most promise as being helpful and relevant for your family? Why?

5. Dr. Taylor recommends to "encourage choice-making." Describe at least three areas in which you could follow through with that recommendation effectively with your child.

6. Document at least one incident in which you enacted each of the four principles for giving filtered help to someone:
   - Help during part of a task
   - Be available when asked
   - Give limited necessary help
   - Give bite-sized help

7. Of the recommendations for "Controlling the Environment," name several ideas that seem worth trying to help your child experience greater personal power.

8. What surprised you the most about this chapter?

9. What were the three most meaningful sentences for you in this chapter?

NOTES

Chapter 1

Eugene Anderson, George Redman, and Charlotte Rogers, *Self-Esteem for Tots to Teens: A Guide for Parents and Teachers* (revised edition); Wayzata, Minnesota: Parenting and Teaching Publications, 1991.

Earl Hipp, *Fighting Invisible Tigers: A Stress Management Guide for Teens* (revised edition); Minneapolis: Free Spirit, 1995.

Gershen Kaufman, Lev Raphael, and Pamela Espeland, *Stick Up for Yourself: Every Kid's Guide to Personal Power and Positive Self-Esteem* (revised edition); Minneapolis: Free Spirit, 1999.

John Taylor, *Answers to A.D.D.: A Practical Guide for Parents*; Warminster, Pennsylvania: Mar-Co, 1997.

John Taylor, *Encouraging the Discouraged Child: Boosting Your Child's Self-Confidence* (revised edition); Warminster, Pennsylvania: Mar-Co, 1995.

John Taylor, *Especially for Helping Professionals: Understanding Parents' Feelings and Emotional Stresses* (audiotape); Salem, Oregon: A.D.D. Plus, 1998.

John Taylor, *Helping Your ADD Child* (revised third edition); Roseville, California: Prima, 2001.

John Taylor, *Motivating the Uncooperative Student*; Warminster, Pennsylvania: Mar-Co, 1990.

John Taylor, *Positive Prescriptions for Negative Parenting* (revised edition); Warminster, Pennsylvania: Mar-Co, 1995.

John Taylor, *The Attention Deficit Hyperactive Student at School* (revised edition); Warminster, Pennsylvania: Mar-Co, 1995.

John Taylor, *Understanding Misbehavior: Using Misbehavior as a Guide to Children's and Adolescents' Needs*; Warminster, Pennsylvania: Mar-Co, 1993.

Chapter 2

Diane Heacox, *Up from Underachievement: How Teachers, Students, and Parents Can Work Together*, Minneapolis: Free Spirit, 1991.

Jean Peterson, *Talk with Teens About Feelings, Family, Relationships, and the Future*, Minneapolis: Free Spirit, 1995.

Jean Peterson, *Talk with Teens About Self and Stress*, Minneapolis: Free Spirit, 1993.

John Taylor, *Diagnostic Interviewing of the Misbehaving Child*, Warminster, Pennsylvania: Mar-Co, 1989.

John Taylor, *Motivating the Uncooperative Student*, Warminster, Pennsylvania: Mar-Co, 1990.

John Taylor, *Understanding Misbehavior: Using Misbehavior as a Guide to Children's and Adolescents' Needs*, Warminster, Pennsylvania: Mar-Co, 1993.

Winnifred Taylor, *Anger Answers: High Impact Interventions for Anger Management and Violence Prevention* (audiotape set); Salem, Oregon: A.D.D. Plus, 1996.

Chapter 3

Miriam Adderholdt and Jan Goldberg, *Perfectionism: What's Bad About Being Too Good?* (revised edition); Minneapolis: Free Spirit, 1999.

Rosemarie Clark, Donna Hawkins, and Beth Vachon, *The School-Savvy Parent: 365 Insider Tips to Help You Help Your Child*, Minneapolis: Free Spirit, 1999.

Suzanne Harrill, *Empowering Teens to Build Self-Esteem*, Houston: Innerworks, 1993.

Barbara Lewis, *Being Your Best: Character Building for Kids 7–10*, Minneapolis: Free Spirit, 2000.

Susanna Palomares, Sandy Schuster, and Cheryl Watkins, *The Sharing Circle Handbook: Topics for Teaching Self-Awareness, Communication, and Social Skills*, Torrance, California: Innerchoice, 1992.

John Taylor, *Correcting Without Criticizing: The Encouraging Way to Talk to Children About Their Misbehavior* (revised edition); Warminster, Pennsylvania: Mar-Co, 1995.

John Taylor, *Creative Answers to Misbehavior: Getting Out of the Ignore-Nag-Yell-Punish Cycle*; Warminster, Pennsylvania: Mar-Co, 1992.

John Taylor, *Encouraging the Discouraged Child: Boosting Your Child's Self-Confidence* (revised edition); Warminster, Pennsylvania: Mar-Co, 1995.

John Taylor, *Listening for Feelings: Helping Children Express Emotions in a Healthy Way* (revised edition); Warminster, Pennsylvania: Mar-Co, 1995.

John Taylor, *No More Sibling Rivalry! Increasing Harmony by Helping Your Children Become Better Friends* (revised edition); Warminster, Pennsylvania: Mar-Co, 1995.

John Taylor, *Nurturing Self-Esteem in ADD/ADHD Children* (audiotape); Salem, Oregon: A.D.D. Plus, 1998.

John Taylor and Winnifred Taylor, *Social Skills Solutions: Strategies for Teaching Children and Teens* (VHS videotape); Salem, Oregon: A.D.D. Plus, 1995.

Chapter 4

Eugene Anderson, George Redman, and Charlotte Rogers, *Self-Esteem for Tots to Teens: A Guide for Parents and Teachers* (revised edition); Wayzata, Minnesota: Parenting and Teaching Publications, 1991.

Carrie Ivey-Cone, *Just for Teens: Speak Out! Get Some Attention* (VHS videotape); Nevada City, California: Ivey-Cone Productions, 1994.

Susanna Palomares, Sandy Schuster, and Cheryl Watkins, *The Sharing Circle Handbook: Topics for Teaching Self-Awareness, Communication, and Social Skills*; Torrance, California: Innerchoice, 1992.

Michele Tamaren, *I Make a Difference: A Curriculum Guide Building Self-Esteem and Sensitivity in the Inclusive Classroom*; Novato, California: Academic Therapy, 1992.

John Taylor, *Listening for Feelings: Helping Children Express Emotions in a Healthy Way* (revised edition); Warminster, Pennsylvania: Mar-Co, 1995.

John Taylor, *Nurturing Self-Esteem in ADD/ADHD Children* (audiotape); Salem, Oregon: A.D.D. Plus, 1998.

Chapter 5

John Taylor, *Correcting Without Criticizing: The Encouraging Way to Talk to Children About Their Misbehavior* (revised edition); Warminster, Pennsylvania: Mar-Co, 1995.

John Taylor, *Creative Answers to Misbehavior: Getting Out of the Ignore-Nag-Yell-Punish Cycle*; Warminster, Pennsylvania: Mar-Co, 1992.

John Taylor, *Diagnostic Interviewing of the Misbehaving Child*; Warminster, Pennsylvania: Mar-Co, 1989.

John Taylor, *Encouraging the Discouraged Child: Boosting Your Child's Self-Confidence* (revised edition); Warminster, Pennsylvania: Mar-Co, 1995.

John Taylor, *Listening for Feelings: Helping Children Express Emotions in a Healthy Way* (revised edition); Warminster, Pennsylvania: Mar-Co, 1995.

John Taylor, *Motivating the Uncooperative Student*; Warminster, Pennsylvania: Mar-Co, 1990.

John Taylor, *Nurturing Self-Esteem in ADD/ADHD Children* (audiotape); Salem, Oregon: A.D.D. Plus, 1998.

John Taylor, *Understanding Misbehavior: Using Misbehavior as a Guide to Children's and Adolescents' Needs*; Warminster, Pennsylvania: Mar-Co, 1993.

Winnifred Taylor, *Anger Answers: High Impact Interventions for Anger Management and Violence Prevention* (audiotape set); Salem, Oregon: A.D.D. Plus, 1996.

Chapter 6

Robert MacKenzie, *Setting Limits: How to Raise Responsible, Independent Children by Providing Clear Boundaries*; Roseville, California: Prima, 1998.

Marguerite Radencich and Jeanne Schumm, *How to Help Your Child with Homework* (revised edition); Minneapolis: Free Spirit, 1997.

Trevor Romain, *How to Do Homework Without Throwing Up*; Minneapolis: Free Spirit, 1997.

John Taylor, *Anger Control Training for Children and Teens: The Adult's Guidebook for Teaching Healthy Handling of Anger* (revised edition); Warminster, Pennsylvania: Mar-Co, 1995.

John Taylor, *Correcting Without Criticizing: The Encouraging Way to Talk to Children About Their Misbehavior* (revised edition); Warminster, Pennsylvania: Mar-Co, 1995.

John Taylor, *Creative Answers to Misbehavior: Getting Out of the Ignore-Nag-Yell-Punish Cycle*; Warminster, Pennsylvania: Mar-Co, 1992.

John Taylor, *Especially for Teachers: Motivating the ADD/ADHD Student* (audiotape); Salem, Oregon: A.D.D. Plus, 1998.

John Taylor, *Helping Hands and Smiling Faces: Getting Cooperation on Household Chores* (revised edition); Warminster, Pennsylvania: Mar-Co, 1995.

John Taylor, *Limits with Love: Effective Discipline Strategies* (audiotape); Salem, Oregon: A.D.D. Plus, 1998.

John Taylor, *No More Tantrums: Anger Control Training* (audiotape); Salem, Oregon: A.D.D. Plus, 1998.

John Taylor, *Understanding Misbehavior: Using Misbehavior as a Guide to Children's and Adolescents' Needs*; Warminster, Pennsylvania: Mar-Co, 1993.

Chapter 7

Terry Beck, *Building Healthy Friendships: Teaching Friendship Skills to Young People*; Saratoga, California: R and E Publishers, 1994.

Pamela Espeland, *Succeed Every Day: Daily Reading for Teens*; Minneapolis: Free Spirit, 2001.

Meredith Gall and Joyce Gall, *Making the Grade: Raise Your Grades by Studying Smarter, Not Harder*; Rocklin, California: Prima, 1993.

Rebecca Greene, *The Teenagers' Guide to School Outside the Box*; Minneapolis: Free Spirit, 2001.

Suzanne Harrill, *Empowering Teens to Build Self-Esteem*; Houston: Innerworks, 1993.

Earl Hipp, *Fighting Invisible Tigers: A Stress Management Guide for Teens* (revised edition); Minneapolis: Free Spirit, 1995.

Gershen Kaufman, Lev Raphael, and Pamela Espeland, *Stick Up for Yourself: Every Kid's Guide to Personal Power and Positive Self-Esteem* (revised edition); Minneapolis: Free Spirit, 1999.

Barbara Lewis, *Being Your Best: Character Building for Kids 7–10*; Minneapolis: Free Spirit, 2000.

Randall McCutcheon, *Get Off My Brain: A Survival Guide for Lazy Students* (revised edition); Minneapolis: Free Spirit, 1998.

Elizabeth Offutt, *An Elementary Teacher's Guide to Multiple Intelligences*; Torrance, California: Good Apple Press, 1997.

Alex Packer, *Highs! Over 150 Ways to Feel Really, Really Good Without Alcohol or Other Drugs*; Minneapolis: Free Spirit, 2000.

Trevor Romain, *Cliques, Phonies, and Other Baloney*; Minneapolis: Free Spirit, 1998.

Jeanne Schumm and Marguerite Radencich, *School Power: Strategies for Succeeding in School* (revised edition); Minneapolis: Free Spirit, 2001.

John Taylor, *Especially for Teens: Shortcuts to School Success* (audiotape); Salem, Oregon: A.D.D. Plus, 1998.

John Taylor, *Living in Harmony: Improving Sibling Relationships* (audiotape); Salem, Oregon: A.D.D. Plus, 1998.

John Taylor, *No More Sibling Rivalry! Increasing Harmony by Helping Your Children Become Better Friends* (revised edition); Warminster, Pennsylvania: Mar-Co, 1995.

John Taylor, *Training in Peacemaking: Improving Social Skills* (audiotape); Salem, Oregon: A.D.D. Plus, 1998.

INDEX